The Construction
of Heritage

DAVID BRETT

CORK
UNIVERSITY
PRESS

First published in 1996 by
Cork University Press
University College
Cork
Ireland

ISBN 1 85918 052 3 hardback
1 85918 053 1 paperback

British Library Cataloguing in Publication Data
A CIP catalogue record for this book is available from the British Library.

Typeset by Seton Music Graphics, Bantry, Co. Cork
Printed by ColourBooks, Baldoyle, Co. Dublin

CONTENTS

ILLUSTRATIONS

All original photographs by Barbara Freeman

1

AN INTRODUCTION

This book investigates the concept of 'heritage': its different meanings, the uses to which it is put, and the places, buildings, institutions and activities that have grown around it. It relates 'heritage' to such topics as the history and development of tourism, sight-seeing, the history of taste, the concept of 'nation' and 'region' and the creation of popular histories. This network of ideas and activities is viewed under the larger heading of *the representation of the past*; that is, how groups, regions and nations view themselves and are viewed by others, as historical entities, and through what tints of which spectacles. The visual connotations are deliberate, since this book is much concerned with issues of visual and architectural representation, and the ideological implications of imagery.

The topic is self-evidently interesting and important. Large numbers of jobs are to be found in something called the 'heritage industry' and this activity is being serviced by courses in 'heritage management'. The concept appears in tourist brochures, in governmental categories, budget-spending heads and even ministries. It bids fair to being a major preoccupation in local government. In areas of poor employment it attracts funding and provides welcome opportunities for advancement. This is not a small matter in any country, but in Ireland, with high general unemployment and areas of acute deprivation, the promotion of local history through theme parks and exhibitions is a useful part of the economy. The future, we may say, is in 'heritage'.

I shall not be offering a definition of the term, since its use has become extremely various and vague. What is meant for the present purposes will become apparent by the examples studied below. My main area of concern, however, will be the relation that the concept 'heritage' has in relation to the activity of history, and to the development of forms of popular, rather than academic or scholarly, history. I shall be analysing a number of instances of 'heritage', and these examples will be mainly Irish.

There are several good reasons for choosing Ireland as the principal field of study, one being that the author lives there, and in its most contested part where there is no common agreement on what constitutes its history, heritage or even name. This book arises directly out of my effort to understand what has been happening around me in the streets of Belfast and the fields of Armagh. Where there is civil conflict, the issue of the representation of the past is more than an academic matter. While this book was being researched seven men and two women were murdered within half a mile of my front door, one acquaintance survived an assassination attempt and another died on active service.

But the example of Ireland has less immediate and more general value. The very confusion between the political and the geographical denotations of 'Northern Ireland' goes to the heart of 'heritage' issues. Whose heritage? Under what description of historical and contemporary reality are we working? The advantages of an extreme case lie in the stark light it sheds on the everyday, for these questions are there to be asked in every instance of representation we encounter. Representations, even in the most benign cases, are never neutral. In the words of Humpty Dumpty, 'Which is to be master – that's all.' How far contending representations can negotiate dialectical alternatives and so produce further and perhaps more 'truthful' understanding is another matter; but the first stage is to become aware of the nature of the representation with which one is faced, and the conventions out of which it is constructed. My analyses are directed to that end.

Ireland is also, in many respects, a representative general example, since its economy depends heavily upon tourism, and the promotion of several kinds of 'heritage' is part of that dependency. That dependency is itself an issue to be considered because it seems to entail a subordinate or peripheral status. In some cases we shall discover that 'peripheral status' has been internalised and assumed. We shall also observe, in some of the closer case studies below, a zone of contest between differing modes and directions of self-definition. I shall argue at several places in this book that 'heritage' is a contemporary mode of popular or non-specialist history, and that the writing or presentation of such histories is always and necessarily contentious. Thus 'heritage' is part of the process of self-definition through historicised self-presentation, and carries with it the signs of contention even when (as is usually the case) those signs have been hidden, ignored, or not noticed. Much of what follows will seek to make explicit the problems lurking in what is usually (but not always) a 'deproblematised' story-telling. This, of course, is not a feature unique to Irish history.

There is a further reason why Ireland is a representative example. The Irish countryside bears everywhere a rich patina of ancient sites, going back to very early periods in European history. For reasons connected with the relative lack of economic development, semi-colonial status, land use and numerous other matters, these sites have remained undisturbed to a degree most unusual in Western Europe. The public consciousness of these sites, their care (or neglect), and their designation as tourist attractions has led to discussion on a considerable scale. They, and the concomitant literature and commentary, have enabled Irish people to claim special access to a large historical territory – Celtic Europe – and to deploy that claim to advantage. The particular character of that antiquity has become a highly marketable cultural commodity in recent years, and the means whereby this has been exploited deserve investigation. Whether or not there is much substantial reality in the notion of 'Celtic Europe' is a matter touched upon from time to time, since if there is little, then some definitions of 'national heritage' need to be altered.[1] Similar questions are (*mutatis mutandis*) there to be asked in many other national and regional situations.

Ireland is also, with some other zones of Europe, a *locus classicus* of the 'unspoilt', the 'picturesque', the 'sublime' and the 'authentic'. An investigation of those terms, which are central to contemporary tourism and the representation of history, could not take place without a discussion of their Irish instantiations. As we shall see below, this discussion again involves a critique of the 'centre–periphery' problem, which is in turn a question of representation. Briefly, Irish commercial tourism presents an 'image' of an essential Ireland to the world that is sharply at variance with Ireland's existential reality, and this state of affairs has existed for a long time. We are led to analyse the distinctions between a national and regional imagery 'for-self' and 'for-others', and to reflect on the degree to which a full self-understanding (whatever that might be) falls through the gap between the two. The same phenomenon is observed, in different disguises, wherever tourism exists. In Ireland's case it is a sharp point of an argument on which to sit, especially where the concept of 'Celticity' is engaged; but once again, Ireland is not a special case, but more of a typical example.

This, too, touches on the degree to which representations of history, culture and 'heritage' have been and are becoming issues and practices around which political forces, frequently malignant, are being organised. I write as someone for whom the experience of living and working in what we must now call 'former Yugoslavia' was a formative experience. In short, the construction (and if need be, the *invention*) of 'heritage' and 'traditions' is part of the political agenda once again in this 'new' Europe which looks at first glance rather like an older Europe of ethnic hatreds. Within the narrower context of Ireland and Northern Ireland in particular, the idea of 'cultural traditions' is used in a very loose way to defuse issues of political

1. The arguments and dilemmas presented by Malcolm Chapman in his book *The Celts: the Construction of a Myth* (London, St Martin's Press 1992) are important here, and reference will be made to them in ch. 5.

2. As will become clear, I am very sceptical about the 'cultural traditions' debate. See Brett, D. 'Material evidence', *Circa*, 62 Autumn 1992 pp. 20–5.

legitimacy.[2] In this respect, our topic deserves the same close and cautious scrutiny we would give to an unexploded bomb.

I think it will be clear from the above that I am not in any way concerned with the establishment or critique of any 'Irish heritage' as such, or any other 'heritage', but rather with the principles that might govern any possible critique in any situation. I do not think I have established those principles, which would require a much larger study than I have been able to make; but I hope that the critical method I adopt will be of preliminary use.

The main thrust of this study will be to treat 'heritage' as a form of popular history. To quote myself:

> History, like art and sport, is not a fixed entity but an activity. History is the story we are constantly telling ourselves to explain to ourselves just how we come to be where we think we are. History, truly considered, is a verb, not an abstract noun. We history. From which it follows that history is not given, but made. The story that we tell ourselves is a form of self-definition and is therefore, and unavoidably, an ethical enterprise. That is why close scholarship is important; it bears a similar relationship to the intellectual life as humility does to the spiritual; it reminds us that we may be in error everywhere. The consequences of fantasy may be lethal. This is also why popular, non-technical historical writing is a serious activity that is very difficult to do well. In so far as heritage attempts to present a popular history in this way, it too must be taken seriously; and we should consider it as one of the forms that a popular history might take today.[3]

3. Brett, in O'Connor, B. and Cronin, M. *Tourism in Ireland: a Critical Analysis* (Cork University Press 1993).

Popular histories, of course, need not always be written, but they will always be narrative – in epic, ballad, theatre, film, and video; and now in the form of spectacle or display, and now again as exhibitions. Nor do we need to draw a precise line between popular and scholarly or academic histories, because the idea of 'popular' is not a location but a direction; it signifies a rhetorical intention, a wide address. The function of a popular history is to create, criticise, assert or defend group memory; and like specialist, academic history it does so through achieving a balance between the analysis of data and imaginative representation. Where that balance is struck is a matter of fine judgements; but I insist that we can speak about the truths of histories, and that these 'truths' involve the critical alignment of datum and representation. It is essential that the alignment be *critical*, that is, reflective upon its own premises, or we mistake the representation alone as the truth, and fail to see its highly mediated and ideological character.

To describe popular history as 'narrative' is to stir a nest of hornets. But since I shall make frequent use of 'narrative' in the critical sections of this book, it is necessary to spend some time on what an historical narrative might be. The very concept of narrative is, when applied to historical data, problematic. The essential question is whether or not the 'narrative' is a feature of the studied reality (one might wish to call this *narrative realism*), or whether or not the narrative is a cognitive device which unifies and makes coherent a mass of data whose interconnections are otherwise very difficult to explain (this would be *heuristic narrative*). Allied to this is the necessarily narrative character of language and the story-telling function inseparable from describing events. The problem has been elegantly summarised by Hayden White:

> Our discourse always tends to slip away from our data towards the structures of consciousness with which we are trying to grasp them: or, what amounts to the same thing, the data always resist the coherency of the image which we are trying to fashion of them.[4]

Some authors have attempted to analyse just what is implied in the idea of 'historical narrative' and have tried to describe the logical rules by which data (which has no necessary order) can be translated into narration (which has).[5] In such arguments, the function of narration is to form meaningful totalities from scattered facts. Others have attempted to classify and give priority to different kinds of narrative and have argued that truth can be predicated not only on simple statements of fact, but on the narrative itself considered as a whole and also as a set of lesser wholes. In this argument, 'truth' is strictly related to the problem of the coherence, integration and integrity of narrative wholes.[6]

Jerzy Topolski makes a useful classification of narrative types to which I shall return in the critical sections of this book. These types, he warns, are ideal constructs which scarcely ever occur in their pure form; any single, existing narrative is likely to be a mix of types. Nevertheless one can make real and meaningful distinctions according to the degree of internal coherence and temporal organisation.

The simplest of all is the *annal*. This typically exists in the form of simple statements in chronological order. 'In this year the Vikings came. They burnt the monastery.' A contemporary Irish example is afforded by the Belfast magazine *Fortnight* which in each issue has listed, without comment, the salient horrors of recent years. In such bald accounts, no general concepts are developed, though the statements in some general sense embody a picture of the world. There is no appeal to previous statements and other known facts. The principle of selection is extremely basic.

The second type is the *chronicle*. This introduces rudimentary ideas of causality and a hierarchy is placed over the facts – some are more important than others. This is significantly more coherent

4. White, Hayden *Tropics of Discourse* (Baltimore, John Hopkins University Press 1978), intro.

5. See Ankersmit, F.R. *Narrative Logic: a Semantic Analysis of the Historian's Language* (The Hague 1983) cited by Topolski, below.

6. I am here paraphrasing Jerzy Topolski 'Historical Narrative: towards a coherent structure', *Beiheft*, 26 History and Theory: Studies in the Philosophy of History.

than the annal, because the reality described includes not only events but also relations between events. In addition, the chronicler knows what has happened before and uses that knowledge; she or he has therefore a time-sense that includes retrospection as well as mere sequence. Thus a structure of explanation becomes possible. Many television documentaries take this form.

The third type is the *scholarly narrative*. Here the writer and reader can look both forward and backward along the direction of time, being both retrospective and prospective; facts are integrated into wholes in terms both of causality and inference, giving an altogether higher level of coherence. Facts are presented in terms of the consequences that flow from them.

These 'horizontal' structures are further qualified by what Topolski calls the 'vertical' strata of any one narrative, of which the deepest layers are the most important. These are concerned with deep principles that control the selection and hierarchisation of the material – the theoretical foundations that may or may not be clearly articulated but which, in whatsoever case, govern the construction of the narrative. This control can itself be controlled only by the exercise of critical method; and since only scholarly narrative admits of this level of self-conscious fashioning, it is there that historical narrative achieves its maximum coherence and integration, or 'truth'. However, all types of narrative have this layered structure and can be analysed in these terms, which will include not only deep theoretical assumptions but also literary and other models, the conventions of representation in other media, and matters left unsaid because it is expected that the reader shares them.

The deep theoretical assumptions of a narrative do not, of course, have to be apparent: 'control by a theory need not mean the articulation by the historian of that theory. It is experienced in the deep stratum as something assumed'.[7] Hayden White, in his far-reaching study of historiography, distinguishes different stages in the creation of historical narratives; the first of these he describes as the 'prefiguration' of the historical field. The historian must 'constitute [the field] as an object of mental perception . . . it must first be construed as a ground inhabited by discernible figures'.[8] This is essentially a poetic and linguistic act which is 'preconceptual'; the field is then conceptualised according to modes of 'emplotment', 'argument' and 'ideological implication', and in accord with the logically necessary 'tropes' of classical and contemporary theories of rhetoric and discourse. This process enables us to turn the data of the historical record into a structure of explanation by way of narrative.

For our purposes these arguments are of value, but a value that must constantly be scrutinised. They treat the task of the historian

7. Topolski, ibid., p. 85.

8. See White, H. *Metahistory: The Historical Imagination in Nineteenth Century Europe* (Baltimore, John Hopkins UP 1973), p. 30.

as the study and creation of *texts*; but we shall be concerned with artefacts, images and architectural space. And while it is certainly true that the creators of heritage museums and centres base their historical research upon texts, what is created and what is experienced by visitors does not easily submit to textual analysis. Objects, pictures, and spaces do not behave in the mind as do words; our experience of them is always in some large measure 'preconceptual'. Thus analysis of an exhibition's narrative can only be *analogous* to the analysis of a narrative in a text, and subject to all the caution that thereby ensues.[9] White, Topolski and other philosophers of history have not addressed themselves to non-literary narratives, though these are common forms of popular history and certainly pre-date prose narrative in its modern form. Nevertheless, the idea of narrative types, and the concept of 'strata', can be employed, carefully, to cover a much wider field. I shall also make extensive use of the notion of 'prefiguration'.

I am going to assume that popular history (whether in text or any other form) lies in a zone between the chronicle and scholarship. It does not normally disclose a self-critical reflection on itself, being usually aimed at confirming given knowledge, but it does seek integration and coherence, and therefore 'truth', rather than merely presenting data. I shall further assume that self-critical disclosure, at the level of popular history as much as at the scholarly, is both possible and desirable because it reveals the mediated and conventional character of whatever form the history takes. This frees the mind. Criticism of popular history (and of 'heritage') will, in its most fundamental respect, be concerned with deep theoretical assumptions, and with bringing them to light. A popular criticism will pursue this aim with maximum clarity and concreteness of example.

This study is concerned particularly with conventions of visual representation, since I argue that these have a formative power over the content of the understanding, and that these conventions are a form of ideology. Here I link *visualisation* to ideology through the concept of 'visual ideology' as developed by Nicos Hadjinicolaou. Though his study is directed toward art history, it provides us with a heading under which to analyse visual displays of other kinds. 'Visual ideology', he writes, 'is the way in which the formal and thematic elements of a picture [*or exhibition etc.*] are combined on each specific occasion. This combination is a particular form of the overall ideology of a social class.'[10] The 'social class' in question will usually be identified through consideration of the clients or commissioning body of a heritage display.

Of equal importance is the narrative structure of a display, which is usually realised through the circulation pattern of the visitors, and by

9. There is, of course, a tendency amongst academic writers to over-emphasise the conceptual structure of their work and to neglect the 'preconceptual' elements of language and in the text's construction. They exhibit an anxiety about pre-conceptuality which is akin to the artist's anxiety about conceptual over-prescription. A more completely theoretical and therefore poetic understanding of narrative, which would grant no special privileges to the literary text, might be arrived at by an equal consideration of all forms of narrational and sequential exposition, without analogy. But not in this book.

10. Hadjinicolaou, N. *Art History and Class Struggle* (London, Pluto Press 1978), p. 95.

the *narrative topology* of sites and buildings, and how we are led from one part to another. We shall also be much occupied with the assumptions underlying different conventions of *simulation* because these (with the other two main headings) are the means whereby non-literary narratives are constructed. The aim will be to examine critically those conventions (and the assumptions embedded in them) in the same spirit as the scholarly historian reveals his or her own governing theoretical foundations. I hope thereby to arrive at a critical method which others will find useful.

Any critical method will direct attention toward the principles of selection involved in any case, not simply the selection of data, nor even the selection of interconnecting arguments ('integration and coherence', 'emplotment', etc.) but also and importantly *the selection of the conventions of representation by which the narrative is brought forward*. This is especially the case where visual representations are concerned; as a problem in what Humphrey Jennings has described as 'imaginary history' – the history of the representations of history. (*See* chapter 2, note 2.)

Here, once more, geographical Ireland is an important example to consider, because there is not an agreed 'national' narrative nor a set of representative strategies around which an unproblematic 'heritage' could be constructed. Indeed, we tend to be obstructed by pseudo-histories and tendentious representations of a very obstinate kind. Principles of selection are partisan; data and representations are frequently at variance, and coherence and integration have, alas, often perished on bitterly contested ground. All nations and geographical regions share these problems, but they rise to the surface very rapidly when the formal political structures of a region are under question, and where geographical unity is challenged by political partition. Issues of the past tend swiftly toward the definition of the present. The representation of the past has a direct bearing upon political legitimacy in the present. Indeed, I shall be arguing, toward the end of this study, that the construction of 'heritage' is a means for the definition of the contemporary, which it reveals in a fantastic or fetishised form.

I shall further argue that 'heritage' is a product of the process of modernisation which, by eroding customs and expectations, forces us to re-articulate our sense of the past; even, in extreme examples, the experience of time itself. Traditional elements of culture and behaviour have to be abandoned and unlearnt before the new mind-set and 'habitus' can be established. By 'habitus' I mean (following Bourdieu) the system of habitual and more or less durable dispositions that defines, without determining, individuals and groups and social classes, and that guides expectations and conduct and taste; all that which assures continuity and regularity even in new situations.[11] Modernity

11. See Bourdieu, P. *The Logic of Practice*, trans. R. Nice (Cambridge, Polity Press 1990), p. 53 and other references. Useful here is the introduction to *The Field of Cultural Practice* (Polity Press 1993) by Randal Johnson.

continually challenges each 'habitus' and the constantly attempted recovery of the past is accordingly a preoccupation of the contemporary present. In popular memory and in imaginative history, the repeated interruptions of modernisation are interpreted as *caesurae* – cutting through the fabric of life. Thereafter, goes my general argument, the past is experienced as a loss or wound, not unlike that of the amputated limb that is still felt long after its removal. This argument is, of course, of a highly generalised and speculative kind, and will be treated with caution; it stands to this short study as an image that 'prefigures' the field.[12] Ireland, in this general sense, came late and unwillingly to the roller-coaster of modernity; what there may be of truth in arguments derived from English or German examples will not fit easily or directly into Irish experience. Nevertheless, the general question of history in its relation to modern experience, and of attempts to reconstitute historical experience back into the present, must be taken first, because the topic under exploration is a concept dependent upon time and the recovery of the past. This will form the substance of the next chapter. One significant conclusion that will arise from this is the inadequacy of the notion of 'post-modernity' to any analysis of 'heritage', despite a common appeal to it by many recent writers.

12. See Brett, D. 'Quantities and Qualities', unpublished Ph.D thesis, Royal College of Art (1984) for the origins of this image.

There is now a considerable growth of literature forming around the concept and practice of tourism, and a branch of this is devoted to heritage. D. Boorstin's *The Image: a Guide to Pseudo-Events in America* (New York, Harper 1964) seems to have been the earliest attempt to develop a modern theory of tourism. It remains a useful book because the guiding concept of the 'pseudo-event' fits very well with more recent studies in the invention of traditions and simulated realities. D. MacCannell both builds on and challenges Boorstin in his *The Tourist: a New Theory of the Leisure Class* (London, Macmillan 1976). He is largely concerned with the pursuit of 'authenticity' which he likens to a quest for the sacred. In this and other writings he develops the idea of a 'staged authenticity' in which the tourists and the toured collude with one another. The relevance of this to our study will be quite clear. His more recent book, *Empty Meeting Grounds; The Tourist Papers* (London, Routledge 1992), develops these arguments and insights very much further as part of a wider study of the movements of peoples. John Urry's *The Tourist Gaze; Leisure and Travel in Contemporary Societies* (London, Sage 1990) contains a useful survey and criticism of these and other writers, and goes on to develop a further account of tourism centred on Foucault's concept of 'the gaze' as an identifying discourse.

The most immediately relevant book would appear to be Robert Hewison's *The Heritage Industry* (London, Methuen 1987). This has the distinction of being addressed directly to our topic, but while some of his arguments and observations are valuable, for our purposes here it is of limited use, being formed around (to quote its own subtitle) 'Britain in a climate of decline'. There is much that may be said about contemporary Ireland, but the word 'decline' does not spring first to mind. Moreover, there are good arguments to suppose that the idea of 'decline' does not fit as neatly as Hewison supposes with the British experience. Urry, in his sixth chapter, entitled 'Gazing on History', makes some telling criticisms of Hewison's notion of 'decline'. He points out that the conservation and historical societies, which are so very large and powerful a force in British life, are frequently of local and popular origins. They are not simply ideological constructs, and they are quite often in conflict one with another.

The explanatory power of 'decline' is weakened by looking beyond these islands and the immediate present. The earliest examples of simulated histories seem to have occurred in the context of national or local self-aggrandisement. As we shall see in chapter 3, the great exhibitions of the nineteenth century, and later, frequently employed what we would now call heritage displays. In the 1900 Paris Exposition International, as part of the celebration of the city's past, an entire *quartier* of 'Old Paris' was built and peopled by salaried inhabitants in medieval costume. Some of the earliest 'heritage parks' of which I am aware are the restored colonial and Independence houses and villages that are quite common in the United States. The role of the Rockefeller family in the creation of 'Williamsburg', or of Henry Ford in the recreation of his own home workshop at Dearborn and those of Edison and the Wright Brothers, are almost paradigm cases in the construction of heritage, yet these are essentially celebratory and didactic, rather than nostalgic. Other American instances make memorials of the Civil War and do not hide the tragic realities; still others make special features of religious or ethnic groups. Though this is a matter that requires further study I do not think that the construction of heritage under these premises could be ascribed to decline. Indeed, in England this does not seem to have been the originating impulse either. A good example would be that of the Castle Museum, York, which in the early 1950s created a street and a square of period shops and workplaces; this came about at the same time as an attempt to tidy up and to modernise the old town with slum clearances and ring roads. It is only during the past fifteen years that the toy-town model has spread out of the museum into the town itself and come to bear down upon it and to create a new/old civic reality. Central York is now dominated by the tourist economy and increasingly resembles its own museum: it is possible to walk through the sixteenth-century alleys around the minster and to think you are indeed within the walls of an exhibition, so antiquarian has the ambience become. For someone who spent much of his early life in the unredeemed city, this is a dismal experience. In this instance we seem to be dealing with a process that began with one set of values and arrived at another.

Different again are the massive programmes of restoration undertaken throughout continental Europe since World War II, to reconstruct whole city centres as they had been before universal destruction. The efforts to rebuild old Frankfurt, Warsaw and Leningrad stand as monuments to national and civic determination not to create a 'living history' but to re-assert the continuity between the past and the living present after the catastrophic caesura of battle.

Urry asks a question which I have taken up independently:

> In the absence of the heritage industry just how is the past normally appropriated? It is certainly not through the academic study of 'history' as such. For many people it will be acquired at best through reading biographies and historical novels. It is not obvious that the heritage industry's account is any more misleading.[13]

Urry then goes on to argue that:

> What does need to be emphasised is that the heritage industry is distorted because of the predominant emphasis on visualisation, on presenting visitors with an array of artefacts, including buildings (either 'real' or 'manufactured') and then trying to visualise the patterns of life that would have emerged around them. This is essentially 'artefactual' history, in which a whole variety of social experiences are necessarily ignored or trivialised, such as war, exploitation, hunger, disease, the law and so on.[14]

The argument of this book, as it develops, will include a critique of visualisation, and the associated simulation. The point to be made in an introductory chapter is that while imagery can and does often 'trivialise' certain social experiences (and certainly from the stance of the text-based historian), these and other social experiences are also inscribed and integrated into the habits and practices of visualisation, and into the artefacts through which they are presented, especially through buildings. The process of inscription and integration is a main theme of the present book.

Urry's discussion of this issue is, unfortunately, far too brief for a study of 'gazing'. It follows that his section on 'Designing for the Gaze' is altogether too cursory, and too dependent upon passing notions of 'post-modernity'. My argument grounds the visualisation of history in the early decades of the nineteenth century, and emphasises the role of visual and architectural simulation. My quarrel with Urry's stimulating book is mainly that for the title we are given very little actual *looking*.

13. Urry, John *The Tourist Gaze; Leisure and travel in Contemporary Societies* (London, Sage 1990), p. 112.

14. Ibid.

In some respects I regard this study as part of a wider intellectual development that investigates the increasingly 'visual' character
of modern society.

Two recent books deal specifically with the Irish dimension to our
subject. *Tourism in Ireland: a Critical Analysis* edited by Barbara
O'Connor and Michael Cronin (Cork University Press 1993)
approaches tourism and heritage from several points of view and with
differing methods. My own contributions to this and to *Culture,
Tourism and Development: the Case of Ireland*, edited by Ullrich
Kockel (Liverpool University Press 1994), significantly rewritten or
re-ordered, form a part of this book. I owe a good deal to my fellow
contributors to these volumes, and to the discussions that have taken
place in conferences and other more informal settings. Other studies
by other authors have also been published.

There is, however, a tendency for writers on tourism to treat the
objects of their study as being more simple than they are. As a coun-
ter to this, I have found Erik Cohen's 'A Phenomenology of Tourist
Experiences' (*Sociology*, 13, 179–99) useful. He attempts to distinguish between five possible modes of tourist experience (recreational,
diversionary, experiential, experimental and existential), defining them
in terms of their differing relations to concepts such as 'the centre',
'strangeness' and 'authenticity'. It is probable (as I shall show from
time to time) that this approach may help us analyse the 'heritage
gaze'. However, the aim of this study is not to assess or analyse what
tourists and heritage-seekers are seeking but to examine what, in fact,
they are *finding*.

Buildings, parks, exhibitions and displays are created by organisations that have their particular values and assumptions inscribed in
their products. These products are prescriptive and normative because
they have been given concrete form; their guiding intentions (conscious or otherwise) can often be quite precisely assessed. A direct
study of the physical manifestations of heritage – quite literally, its
construction – reveals something of the values and ideological functions of the concept.

All these writers and others have helped this study in specific or
more general ways, as have other uncredited authors. But I think it
will be useful to make a further distinction between this existing
literature and my own. With the exception of Robert Hewison, previous writers have been based in the social sciences. I am approaching
'heritage' and its manifestations with a mind informed by design
history, architectural theory, and the practice of art criticism; I make
extensive use of aesthetic concepts, especially in the transference of
the spatial language of tourism to the temporal language of heritage.
In this I concur with David Harvey:

There is much to be learned from aesthetic theory about how different forms of spatialization inhibit or facilitate processes of social change. Conversely, there is much to be learned from social theory concerning the flux and change with which aesthetic theory has to cope. By playing these two currents of thought off against each other, we can, perhaps, better understand the ways in which political–economic change informs cultural practice.[15]

This book also arises, in no small degree, from the concerns, over twelve years, of *CIRCA* art magazine, on whose editorial board I have served. *CIRCA*, through the medium of art critical writing, has pursued what we have termed 'the politics of location'; how, and in what forms, can an indigenous modernity be achieved in Ireland, and what are the specific conditions of work here? What are the natures and roles of visual representations? In what follows I owe a great deal to our editorial debates and the contributions of *CIRCA* writers.

I am also aware, in a more general sense, of the slow-burning influence of situationist theory and Guy Debord's *Society of the Spectacle* (Detroit, Black and Red 1983), of my own doctoral thesis (RCA 1984), and of other writings and influences more or less obscure.

In using the term 'heritage' in this book I have sometimes placed it between quotes in order to signal its problematic character, but I have generally only done so in the first stages of an argument, so as not to overload the typography.

15. Harvey, D. *The Condition of Postmodernity; an Enquiry into the Origins of Cultural Change* (Oxford, Blackwell 1989), p. 207.

2

A PREOCCUPATION WITH THE PAST:
Modernity and the Sense of Time

Colin Sorenson has remarked on

> an almost universal . . . preoccupation with 'the past'. This is not so much an interest in history, which one might understand as an awareness of the process of cause and effect in some sort of chronological sequence, but much more an urgent wish to achieve an immediate confrontation with a moment in time, a re-entry into vanished circumstance . . . [in which] 'real', physical, audible and (especially popular) smellable realities of a distant 'then' become a present and convincing 'now'.[1]

1. Colin Sorenson 'Theme Parks and Time Machines', in Vergo, P. (ed.) *The New Museology* (London, Reaktion Books 1989).

I shall return to this passage later, and to the idea of an 'immediate confrontation', and to the image of 're-entry'. But it is not simply the past that is brought forward into the present, but ourselves that are transported back into the past. Movement in space is translated into movement in time. This is perfectly expressed in a brochure introducing the Ulster–American Folk Park, near Omagh, Northern Ireland.

> Sail away to the New World on the brig *Union* and meet us at work in our kitchens and farms.
> Stroll around the grounds of the Ulster–American Folk Park and enjoy a few hours of living history. Visit the authentically-furnished thatched cottages of Rural Ulster and the log cabins of frontier America and you will be sure of a warm welcome from our costumed interpreters as they busy themelves at their everyday tasks. Turf fires, the aroma of baked bread and the clicking of the spinning wheel all contributed to the special atmosphere of bygone days. You will learn a great deal about the lives of the thousands of men, women and children who left in the eighteenth and nineteenth centuries to seek their fortunes in the New World of America.
> You can even travel with them on board the emigrant ship and experience the sounds, smells and dreadful conditions of life at sea.
> (Ulster–American Folk Park Brochure from 1992)

Many other such examples could be cited, in which the language of tourism is being transferred from travel in space to travel in time. I propose that we cannot understand the idea of heritage without examining what it is possible to mean by such persuasive notions as a distant *then* becoming a present *now*; and how the bringing of the past into the present requires a strategy whereby time is given spatial form in a place.

Most discussion of heritage and temporal tourism has been conducted in an intellectual context created by ideas of 'post-modernity', and in the belief that simulated pasts are a recent phenomenon. But I believe it will be much more useful to set the topic of heritage against the formation of industrial modernity in the longer and broader term. This is because an articulate anti-modernism and a preoccupation with the past is coeval with modernity and because, from the very first, the violent and painful processes of primary industrialisation were accompanied by an idealisation of imagined pasts. Great efforts were made to achieve that 're-entry into vanished circumstances', and this preoccupation could and did exist simultaneously with radical innovation, even in the same mind.

Allied to this, in ways that vary from one country to another, is a concern with 'national character' observable all through the nineteenth century as part of the process of nation-building. The ancient pasts of peoples could be invoked to direct the future, and where those ancient pasts were obscure or ambiguous, more acceptable versions could be synthesised or even invented and then represented to the world as 'traditions'. Such traditions had the task of providing norms in a world without normality, to assert a continuity that daily experience denied.

I propose that the preoccupation with the past is created out of the experience of continual change; it comes into being as its dialectical counterpart, born of the stress experienced when one social 'habitus' is being replaced by another. Far from being a symptom of a supposed 'post-modernity', the preoccupation with the past, and the typical means for evoking it, lie in the very foundations of modernity.[2]

In so arguing I shall be drawing upon British and other examples which do not always have an easy or direct reference to most Irish cases, but my aim is to construct a logical architecture, a house of theory, in which to be able to think about the problem. I shall also be advancing an argument about the nature of modernisation which will be open to several lines of empirical criticism; briefly, I propose a fairly conventional 'catastrophic' model of incremental and self-augmenting innovation – a history of leaps forward countered by backward glances. The empirical objections to this model are appropriate to social, economic and technological histories, but much less so to our present business because the intention here is to develop what Humphrey Jennings has described as 'imaginative history'; that is to say the history of representations.[3]

2. I hope that, in a book of this scope, I shall be forgiven for not engaging in a detailed discussion of 'modernity'. The position taken here is similar to that taken by David Harvey in his *The Condition of Post Modernity* (Oxford, Basil Blackwell 1989) – cited elsewhere in these pages. The general form of my argument (its 'prefiguration') derives from my own doctoral thesis (RCA 1984) and it confirms McCandless's observation that: 'The progress of modernity ['modernisation'] depends on its very sense of instability and inauthenticity. For moderns, reality and authenticity are thought to be elsewhere: in other historical periods and other cultures, in purer, simpler lifestyles. In other words, the concern of moderns for 'naturalness', their nostalgia and their search for authenticity are not merely casual and somewhat decadent, though harmless, attachments to the souvenirs of destroyed cultures and dead epochs. They are also components of the conquering spirit of modernity – the grounds of its unifying consciousness.' (McCandless 1976 p. 3)

3. Jennings, H. *Pandaemonium: The Coming of the Machine as seen by Contemporary Observers* (London, Andre Deutsch 1985).

During the 1840s it was possible for a single individual to be both modern and anti-modern at the same time. An enthusiasm for all matters medieval dominated the formal culture of the period, and can be seen in architecture, painting, the applied arts, literature and social customs; this co-existed with the maximum forward drive of industrial capitalism at its most rapacious and a belief in 'political economy'.

This enthusiasm took form in literature first. The development of the popular historical novel is, quite clearly, an element in the longer-term construction of heritage, and though literature is not a central concern of this study, some time must be spent in the company of Walter Scott and his successors. A writer in *Bentley's Miscellany* (1859) wrote, in words familiar to any theme-park publicist, that the attraction of historical fiction lay

> Not in any facility which it affords for the construction of a better story, nor any superior interest that attaches to the known and prominent characters with which it deals, or to the events it describes: but rather the occasion it gives for making us familiar with the every-day life of the age and country in which the scene is laid.[4]

4. *Bentley's Miscellany Vol. XLV* (1859) p. 44. Quoted by Sanders, A. in *The Victorian Historical Novel 1840–1880* (London, Macmillan 1978), p. 15.

Scott's importance and immense skill lay not in his historical insight but in the close-meshed description of the texture of past lives imaginatively re-created for the present – a kind of 'immediate confrontation'. This was not only in a gift for character, but also in an attitude to the different registers of Scots and English speech. National and regional differences were used, not to establish superiorities or polish stereotypes, but to give a credible thickness and richness to his stories.[5] His central characters, in their ordinariness, invited his readers' fanciful relocation of themselves into the characters' pasts. His ideological importance lay in the imaginative foundations that he laid for a broad and general non-partisan conservatism, which produced a British popular history for the nineteenth century – a story in which contending extremes always had to meet, eventually, in social compromise. A recent writer argues that Scott 'established a pattern of accounting for social change, and explaining even comparatively recent changes to a world that was beginning to lose touch with its past'.[6]

5. For a short discussion of this theme, see Kelly, G. *English Fiction of the Romantic Period 1789–1830* (London, Longman 1989), pp. 147–9.

6. Sanders, op. cit., p. 11.

His main theme, at least in the 'Waverley' novels, is the acceptance of progress, professionalisation and modernity; yet the stories rise out of backgrounds of violence, disunity, civil and religious intolerance.[7] The appeal of this conceptual movement toward nineteenth-century moral and intellectual norms was immense, and when coupled with his concrete realism (much more apparent then than now), it provided a fictional template against which real social manners could develop, for good or ill.

7. See Kelly, op. cit., ch. 5.

The novelist's influence on the development of 'Scottish heritage' has been studied by a number of writers, not least H. Trevor Roper, whose essay on the 'Highland tradition' is both exemplary and malicious.[8] As president of the Celtic Society of Edinburgh, Scott was in charge of the ceremonials on the occasion of George IV's visit to the Scottish capital in 1822, on which occasion the 'Highland tradition' of kilts and clan tartans was initiated. 'Do come,' he wrote to an acquaintance, 'and bring half-a-dozen or half-a-score of clansmen, so as to look like an island chief, as you are . . . Highlanders are what he [the king] will best like to see.'[9] Thus the move toward a 'modern' Scotland was balanced by a counter-move to invent a 'primitive' past.[10]

It is to Scott's credit that he attempted later to unmask the wilder aspects of the Highland cult and its element of complete fraudulence; but it illustrates the contemporary power of his historical imagination, which was in evidence yet again with the publication of *Ivanhoe* (1820) and the subsequent attempts to revive the idea of chivalry.

The enthusiasm for tournaments and similar feudal pastimes has been studied in some detail by Mark Girouard.[11] Neo-medieval fancy-dress, balls, elaborate tournaments and masquerades were a remarkable feature of high-society life in the 1830s and '40s.

While the precise 'visual ideology' involved in this knowing simulation requires much more study, there is no doubt that those most concerned with capitalist modernisation were at one and the same time those most involved in the evocation of its exact opposite.

Henry Brougham, the leading Whig politician and an associate of the radical faction, was an enthusiast for jousting, staged knightly festivals in full medieval costume, and had his family home in Westmoreland reconstructed in 'feudal style'. Daniel Maclise, a passionately involved painter of historic scenes (and much concerned with inventing images of Ireland's ancient past), was a member of the editorial board of *The Journal of Design and Manufactures*, a publication devoted to the reform of industrial design and edited from the very centre of cultural modernisation. The Prince Consort himself, whom one might wish to describe in other respects as a futurist, appeared in medieval dress at a court ball in 1842, had himself painted in armour in 1844, and was buried under an effigy of himself as a crusader knight.[12] Richard Cobden exclaimed that:

> We have the spirit of feudalism rife and rampant in the midst of the antagonistic development of the age of Watt, Arkwright and Stevenson! . . . So great is its power and prestige that it draws to it the support and homage of even those who are the natural leaders of the newer and better civilisation.[13]

8. Trevor-Roper, H. 'The Highland Tradition of Scotland', in Hobsbawn, E. and Ranger, T. (eds.) *The Invention of Tradition* (Cambridge UP 1983). Malicious, because the author displays no understanding of the cultural damage against which the invention of traditions is a reaction.

9. Ibid., p. 30. See *Letters of Sir W. Scott VII* p. 213.

10. But see also a more subtle critique by Malcolm Chapman in his *The Celts: the Construction of a Myth* (London, St Martin's Press 1992) pp. 138–42.

11. See Girouard, M. *Return to Camelot: Chivalry and the English Gentleman* (London, Yale UP 1981).

12. For discussion, see Girouard, M., ibid. And for the prince consort as a futurist, see Brett (1984).

13. Wiener, M. J. *English Culture and the Decline of the Industrial Spirit 1850–1980* (Cambridge UP 1981), p. 14.

The simulation of supposedly medieval attitudes and design styles was, in fact, a major cultural activity.

The taste for the medieval both required and was intensified by serious historical and archaeological study of a factual, positivist, character; that is to say, the design research into costume, applied arts and building was modern in nature, even while its enthusiasms were antiquarian. It is in fact the precision of the research that made this kind of design archaeology a part of the larger project of the modernisation that it appears to reject. Nowhere is this more cleary seen than in the architectural and design work of A.W. Pugin and his followers.

This is not the place to repeat architectural history, but no other individual did more than Pugin (with his patrons) to give built form to neo-medievalism. To enter a church such as St Giles, Cheadle (1842–3), or a hall such as those at Scarisbrick Hall (1838) or Alton Castle (1848) is to make that 're-entry into vanished circumstances' with astonishing force. Pugin's designs were informed in every part by his learned, even obsessional, attention to the detail of real medieval design and construction; but he was not a maker of simulacra;

> We do not wish to produce mere servile imitations of former excellence of any kind, but men imbued with the consistent spirit of the ancient architects, who would work on their principles, and carry them out as the old men would have done, had they been placed in similar circumstances, and with similar wants to ourselves . . . We do not want to revive a facsimile of the works or style of any particular individual, or even period . . . it is not a style, but a principle.[14]

14. Pugin, A. W. *An Apology for a Work Entitled 'Contrasts'* (1837).

He was, indeed, looking to reconstruct an imagined past, what he called 'a Catholic Utopia', peopled with renovated human beings.

This imagined past took on polemical form in the publication of *Contrasts* in 1836. The subtitle reads: 'A parallel between the noble edifices of the fourteenth and fifteenth centuries, and similar buildings of the present day; shewing the present decay of taste.' It consists principally of paired illustrations; a 'Catholic Town of 1440' is contrasted with 'The Same Town in 1840' – to the latter's great disadvantage. 'Contrasted residences for the poor' set a panoptical workhouse in brutal contrast with a humane and richly worked alms-house. In every case the style of drawing and *mise-en-page* underpinned the message; the idealised past was set against a brutalising present. The book made no pretence to 'accuracy'; it was modern image-propaganda of the most effective and durable kind, copied ever afterwards by every proponent of change. It was an attempt to rewrite history, to erase Reformation, neoclassicism and the Enlightenment. (In Hayden White's terms, Pugin was engaged in a radical 'prefiguration' of the field.)

But at the same time this imagined past was being brought forward as a possible present, and it was to be achieved by contemporary means. Pugin's enormous personal endeavour, which was itself only a small part of a vast contemporary building programme, could only be realised by industrial methods. A typical example is the close collaboration between Pugin and the firm of Minton, whose floor and wall tiles are the ubiquitous mark of nineteenth-century domesticity. The antiquarian demands of the architect met the technological passion of the manufacturer and a medieval craft was mechanised. The manufacture of high-quality furnishings and architectural fittings of every kind was stimulated by the Gothic revival for trade at home and round the world. The collection of real medieval artefacts that Pugin made for his workmen to copy as they worked on rebuilding the Houses of Parliament became the archetypes for millions of industrial and semi-industrial reproductions.[15]

The rebuilt Houses of Parliament (from 1836) deserves the attention of the student of heritage, since it embodies most of the themes examined in these pages. It is a visual representation of a concept of the state, an example of visual ideology of the most obvious and public kind, and its imagery promotes an interpretation of history that is, at least, tendentious. The geometry of Charles Barry's plan, accepted partly on the strength of Pugin's draughtsmanship, symbolised an ideal two-chambered constitution which was already superseded; since the Reform Acts of the previous decade, power was passing with increasing speed to the Commons. The imagery of Pugin's façades and interiors, spreading relentlessly like some stone and timber ivy over Barry's symmetrical plan and adventurous elevation, blends with the real medieval elements and produces a structure whose eccentricity is hidden from us by daily familiarity. The medieval/royalist emblems and symbology of the decoration could only have been acceptable to an official patronage that shared, or was at least willing to collude in, the fantasy of a vanished *then* brought into a present *now*.[16]

15. The most complete account easily available is Atterbury, P. and Wainwright, C. (eds.) *Pugin: A Gothic Passion* (Yale UP with the V. & A. Museum, Newhaven and London 1994).

16. Moreover, as the century progressed it entrenched itself in state ceremonial: 'In an essentially static age, unchanging ritual might be a genuine reflection of, and reinforcement to, stability and consensus. But in a period of change, conflict or crisis, it might be deliberately unaltered so as to give an impression of continuity, community and comfort, despite overwhelming contextual evidence to the contrary.' (Cannadine, D. 'The Context, Performance and Meaning of Ritual: The British Monarchy and the "Invention of Tradition" *c.* 1820–1977', in Hobsbawn and Ranger (eds.) (1983) p. 105.)
David Cannadine has shown that in the earlier part of the century, state (and especially royal) ceremonial occasions were sparsely attended, ineptly organised and of little significance: 'To put it in the language of the anthropologist, these London-based displays in this early period did not articulate a coherent ceremonial language, as had been the case in Tudor and Stuart times, and was to happen again toward the end of the nineteenth century.' (op. cit., p. 116)

2.1 A.W. Pugin. The Palace
of Westminster (from 1845);
details of stonework.

In the case of William Burges (whose church at Studley Royal is
discussed briefly in the case studies in chapter 5), the medieval was
assimilated into the modern in a particularly striking fashion:

> The distinguishing characteristics of the Englishman of the nineteenth
> century are our immense railway and engineering works, our line-of-
> battle ships, our good and strong machinery . . . our free constitution,
> our unfettered press and trial by jury . . . No style of architecture can

be more appropriate to such a people than . . . [early French Gothic] . . . which is characterised by boldness, breadth, strength, sternness and virility.[17]

Perhaps the highest point reached in this fantasia was the extravagant building programme of Ludwig II of Bavaria, whose castles mark the point at which shared public fantasia passes over into individual lunacy.[18] But there were many gradations on this scale. A notable Irish example is Dromore Castle, designed by E.W. Godwin for the Earl of Limerick, and built in 1868–70. This is a transcription of the cathedral and tower on the Rock of Cashel in Tipperary, which nevertheless contained the most up-to-date modern services.

It was once normal to deride nineteenth-century neo-medievalism as a flight from reality, but this is as mistaken as the more recent attempts to celebrate it as 'high camp'. What we are looking at is the creative fantasy of a dominant class profoundly unsure of its authenticity and cultural grounding, and using reconstructions of the past to define or construct norms for the present; it is clearly and unmistakably an almost paradigm case of 'visual ideology'. And those who developed the fantasy to its heights were *as we might expect* amongst those most profoundly conscious of the cultural dislocation that underlay the fantasy.

The combination of scholarship and retrospection, with a determination to bend the present to the past, passes from Pugin into the arts and crafts movement. Once again, there is only space to present this argument in a foreshortened form, but it serves to root the questions of heritage still more firmly in the nineteenth century and the stresses of primary industrialisation.

In 1862 Warrington Taylor, William Morris's business manager, wrote to his chief that 'You don't want any style, you want something English in character . . . the test of good work would be absence of style.' But what Taylor believed to be 'English' was something at variance with the actually existing state of the country, now rapidly progressing toward full industrialisation:

> Everything English, except stockjobbing London and cotton Manchester, is essentially small, and of a homely farmhouse kind of poetry . . . above all things nationality is the greatest social trait, English Gothic is small as our landscape is small, it is sweet, picturesque, homely, farmyardish . . .[19]

As distinct from Pugin, whose ideal prototypes were the learned and technically advanced buildings of the fifteenth century, the ideals of the arts and crafts movements (both in Britain and all over Europe – under strong British influence) were fixed (one almost writes 'fixated') upon a supposed vernacular *character*. We find, during the 1870s, the construction of these ideas into an orthodoxy summed

From the 1870s onward, however, the position of the head of state was ceremonially advanced both in ritual, spectacle and its mediation through the press, and eventually radio and television. This was done through the recreation as rituals of events that had hitherto been perfunctory – such as the state opening of parliament, through an immense elaboration and dignification of the coronation service, and through staged celebration such as the diamond jubilee.

17. See Crook, Mordaunt J. *The Dilemma of Style: Architectural Ideas from the Picturesque to the Postmodern* (London, Murray 1987), p. 83. (This book is a fine introduction to some of these problems.)

18. Ludwig's palace at Linderhof contains neo-baroque interiors by Franz von Leitz, who was famous for his theatre sets and was director of the Munich State Theatre. Down in the basement is a 'Grotto of Venus' (designed by Fidelis Schabet in 1875), inspired by the music of Wagner, which includes an illuminated lake, swans, murals, arrangements for music and a little boat in which the king could be transported into another world. The castle of Neuschwanstein (1869–81) was conceived as the embodiment of legendary history.

19. Girouard, M. *Sweetness and Light: the Queen Anne Movement 1860–1900* (Oxford, Clarendon Press 1977), p. 18.

up by writers such as W.G. Collingwood, in which 'an honest handful of tradesmen and farmers, and a decent lot of labouring men' might sustain a 'spontaneous art-instinct'. Only such could create 'domestic ornament of an unpretending but thoroughly artistic sort'.[20] This was rooted in the belief that 'in secluded villages . . . untaught genius has created native styles and schools of carving and pottery not unworthy of serious commendation'. Furthermore, 'A real national style can only exist when the people produce it, and when the people enjoy it; it can only exist when the people have artistic, as opposed to mechanical lives.'[21] But this neo-vernacular impulse is in fact detaching its village models from their real historical character, and representing them as being in some sense 'timeless' and 'ethnic' when, correctly understood, the vernacular no less than the learned is the product of change, economics, technology and ownership.

Another outcome of the arts and crafts movement was a desire to defend existing monuments from excessive and ignorant restoration, in order to preserve the results of that 'art-instinct'. The Society for the Protection of Ancient Buildings (f. 1877), of which Morris was the first secretary, established the principle of 'repair, not restoration'. John Ruskin had argued twenty years earlier that there is

> no question of expediency or feeling whether we shall preserve the buildings of past times or not. *We have no right whatever to touch them.* They are not ours. They belong, partly to those who built them, and partly to all the generations of mankind who are to follow us.[22]

The society was the progenitor of all subsequent movements to protect 'our architectural heritage', leading in time to the designation of 'listed buildings', to the country house policy of The National Trust, and to parts of planning legislation. Not surprisingly, the political orientation of the society was poised rather uneasily between radical interventionism and a resentment of the new.

The idea of national character, of an essential 'Englishness', 'Irishness', etc., and its expression in building and craft, (an idea that is central to the arts and crafts movements right across Europe), is clearly and consciously related to the idea of the 'picturesque', which I investigate in the next chapter. It is connected through rural imagery, through the belief in vernacular virtues (actually a modernised version of the pastorale) and in a typical delight in variability and balanced asymmetry. Houses such as Phillip Webb's 'The Red House', built for Morris in 1859, should be understood as (amongst several other matters) attempts to reify a 'character' and through that a 'history'. Even more vivid examples were created later by architects such as M.H. Baillie Scott and Edwin Lutyens; these set the pattern for

20. Collingwood, W.G. *The Philosophy of Ornament* (Orpington, George Allen 1883), pp. 224–5.

21. Ibid., p. 208.

22. Ruskin, J. *Collected Works.* Vol. 36. (Orpington, George Allen, 1904), p. 239.

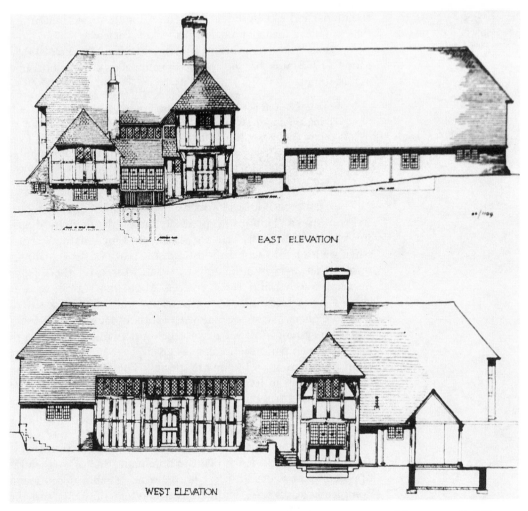

EAST ELEVATION

WEST ELEVATION

countless 'Tudorbethan' commercial developments that continue down to the present day.

Houses such as these – richly textured, allusive, asymetric and deliberately archaic in their formal language – are the late products of the 'picturesque' implications of Ruskin's theories, and the long-standing ruralism that lay behind them. Ideas of this kind remain powerful, and have been skilfully synthesised with 'modernism' by architects such as Edward Cullinan, whose visitor centre at Studley Royal is discussed in chapter 5.

The ideal of a national character or style existed also in music. At its simplest this consisted in Hubert Parry's flat assertion that 'style is ultimately national'.[23] Folk-song in particular was superior to other music because it was not the creation of a limited individual but 'a

2.2 A preoccupation with the past. M. H. Baillie Scott: Village Hall, Iwerne Minster, Dorset. Elevation drawings from *The Architect*, 29 August, 1920.

23. Vaughan Williams, R. *National Music and other Essays* (London, Oxford UP 1963), p. 2.

24. Sharp, C. *English Folk Song;*
Some Conclusions (private
printing 1907), p. x.

communal and racial product, the expression, in musical idiom, of aims and ideals that are primarily national in character'.[24]

Vaughan Williams's principal contention in his essay on 'National Music' (1932) was that the essence of national quality will be found in folk-song:

> In fact, if we did not know from actual experience that there was such a thing as folk-song we should have to imagine it theoretically. But we do find the answer to this inquiry in real fact. The theoretical folk-singer has been discovered to be an actuality. We really do find these unlettered, unsophisticated, and untravelled people who make music which is often beautiful in itself and has in it the germs of great art.[25]

25. Vaughan Williams,
op. cit., p. 15.

There is a circular logic at work here whereby the idea of a national style (in this case, musical) is predicated upon the theoretical postulate of the folk artist. That we actually find such 'natural' artists when we look for them demonstrates the truth of the initial premise – that style is ultimately national. Moreover, there is, as he admits, something 'self-conscious' about this search, yet it is also a secret, a birthright, an 'unconscious' which cannot be shared with foreigners. We are dealing with a form of tautology, or a self-affirming system. And we are also being drawn into a system of ideas in which nations are taken as given, have no historicity, are almost as natural as biological species. These nations have an 'essence' which in its recesses is unknowable by outsiders. It is therefore not a truly historical phenomenon at all, but a cultural inheritance of a genetic kind, that resists change. It is indeed a heritage in a quasi-biological sense.

So deep and extensive was this anti-industrial reaction that it seems at times to have formed the dominant tone of English (as opposed to the wider British) culture, forming habits of sentiment completely at variance with the real conduct of affairs and the active life of the inhabitants.[26] At the same time, as we shall note shortly, we must be on our guard against describing this movement of feeling and taste as being in some obvious sense 'anti-modernist'. What now appears to be 'modernism' in retrospect is only that aspect of a cultural phase that has managed to survive intact into the present. In their time, Pugin, Ruskin and Morris and their very many associates and followers were proposing an alternative reading of history that would act as a template for the building of an alternative future.

26. For discussion,
see Wiener op. cit.

Whereas in England we can see the anti-modern reaction as a dominant cultural atmosphere, in Germany, from a rather later date, the reaction was identified most closely with the so-called 'Mittelstand', a distinct and formally recognised class of self-employed workpeople and skilled artisans. This small but substantial political entity was economically and socially damaged by the speed of German industrialisation in the 1870s and later. Shulamith Volkov has observed that they developed a 'general social resentment and a hostility toward everything modern . . . often vague and confused, but at the same time radical and powerful'. This popular anti-modernism, she concludes, 'was the mental response of men who found themselves overwhelmed by material hardship and social pressure . . . suffering a sense of homelessness and desperately trying to overcome it'.[27]

27. Volkov, S. *The Rise of Popular Anti-Modernism in Germany; the Urban Master Artisans, 1873–1896* (Princeton UP 1978), p. 299, p. 326.

> Perhaps the most powerful link among the small urban craftmasters was a consciousness of their shared past. The memory of the Guild Age was a vital factor in making them into a modern social group. This collective memory had little to do with the actual history of the craft guilds. It was a mythical view of a historical period relegated to an indefinite past. It was faithfully preserved by the master craftsmen, repeated endlessly in public lectures and at artisans' clubs, reiterated in numerous articles in their newspapers and at practically all their local and national meetings . . . Curiously, every generation of artisans during the nineteenth century claimed that the ruin of this ideal past was part of its unique experience. Even at the end of the century the masters still insisted that they had experienced something of that glorious time in their youth. This imagined memory was eventually turned into a powerful ideological and organizational tool by men probably deluded by their own propaganda. It may have had little to do with their historical past, but it certainly became a fundamental instrument for shaping their future.[28]

28. Ibid., p. 23.

Under such pressures, handcraft came to be identified with national culture, and national culture with rural and small-town models. 'Handwork is freedom, morality and justice. Those who are against handwork are in fact standing against freedom, against morality, against justice.'[29] This anti-modern sentiment became part of a much larger 'Heimat' tendency, which was conceived as a 'lebensreform' – a reform of national life tending toward the assertion of a particular German identity in the face of the growing internationalisation of culture. The architect Heinrich Tessenow wrote in 1919:

29. In *Deutsche Handwerker Zeitung*, 10 Feb. 1894, cited by Volkov, p. 30.

> Ultimately our children will build us as craftsmen a world of small towns that will be characterised by great external modesty and yet be the products of the highest skill – a world so rich and splendid that nothing can compare with it.[30]

30. In *Das Hohe Ufer*, 1, 1919.

These yearnings were part of the soil from which the Nazi movement grew. Opposed to this was a 'modernist' tendency summed up best in Herman Muthesius's address to the Deutsche Werkbund in 1914:

> For as our life is becoming international, a certain uniformity of architectural forms will spread across the globe. We have this uniformity

31. For discussion see Campbell, J. *The German Werkbund; the Politics of Reform in the Applied Arts* (Princeton UP 1978), p. 10.

already in our dress. From pole to pole people wear the same jacket and the same blouse. Associations for the conservation of folk dress will not alter this tendency, nor will movements to conserve folk art stand in the way of the internationalisation of forms.[31]

Volkov's account of the 'mittelstand' reaction is interesting. She describes the urban craftmasters as 'anti-modern' but also as being constituted as a modern social group *by their adherence to a myth*, to an 'imagined memory' which became a 'fundamental instrument for shaping their future'. Taking this with what we have noted as the ambivalent face of neo-medievalism, and with our other examples, it is no longer sufficient to describe the backward glance of nineteenth-century culture as reactionary, escapist or anti-modern. We are compelled to think of it is as integral to the experience of modernisation, and to see a full 'modernity' as including what appears to be its opposite. A modern culture (and I propose this as a general rule) is always Janus-faced, looking both backward and forward, never fully settled in the present.

The Barry–Pugin design for the Palace of Westminster was chosen because the Gothic style was believed, by the parliamentary committee, to be peculiarly *English*. (That the same claim was advanced for Gothic in both Germany and France seemed to worry nobody.) This belief in 'national character' and attempts to realise it in buildings and spectacle ran all through the later part of the nineteenth century. It took on particular importance in the smaller nations of Europe, where, for want of political channels, 'national culture' became part of a revolutionary ideology.

But the very survival of national and local culture was perceived as a problem of scholarship and preservation. Ralph Wornum, commenting on the problems of style revealed in the Great Exhibition of 1851, wrote that

> The time has now gone by, at least in Europe, for the development of any particular or national style, and for this reason it is necessary to distinguish the various tastes that have prevailed through past ages, and preserve them as distinct expressions, or otherwise, by using indiscriminately all materials, we should lose all expression . . . if all . . . is to degenerate into a uniform mixture of all elements, nothing will be beautiful.[32]

32. Wornum, R. *The Exhibition as a Lesson in Taste*, Ill. Cat. of the Gt. Exhibition, 1851.

Thus from around this date, varying according to local imperatives and opportunities, we find scholars, architects and artists studying, recording and paraphrasing peasant and regional arts with a view to sustaining 'distinct expressions'.

The case of Hungarian cultural nationalism is instructive, since the idea of a 'distinct expression' was grounded in a highly distinct language and history. There, as in many other smaller nations, the art and culture of the peasantry was seen as preserving ancient cultural forms, which in turn could provide templates for a new national culture, should that become politically feasible. 'Art works were needed with popular themes and motifs and symbolic character for the visual representation and spreading of the newly conceived folk-national ideology.'[33] Vernacular forms and motifs were held to embody the essence of national character. 'The extremely rich and still living folk arts were considered as the *vocabulary* of a "mother-tongue of forms" in their motifs and as a *grammar* of this language in their use of materials, construction and environmental and social connections.'[34] The difficulty here was that there existed a serious and ideologically loaded differentiation between the 'European' (progressive) and 'Oriental'(conservative) definitions of Hungarian language and culture (a debate that continues down to this day):

> The search for the actual implementation of the vernacular has never been completely accepted as a tool for national progress, for 'national' and 'progress' are considered as contradictory, incompatible ideas. The imposed choice has been between being *national*, interpreted on one hand as: conservative, provincial, isolated; or *progressive*, interpreted on the other hand as: unpatriotic, cosmopolitan, imitative.[35]

From this dilemma sprang two architectural traditions, one intensely concerned with preserving continuity at the expense of novelty, and another using 'national' motifs scenographically, as signs of modernity. But in both cases an essentialist cultural/national theory is at work, asserting that there is a permanent, ahistorical national character.

The Hungarian search for a 'mother-tongue of forms' can be paralleled *mutatis mutandis* throughout Europe. In other situations the challenge of a national distinct expression could be met by synthesising from an existing array of village styles. The case of Smetana's opera *The Bartered Bride* (1866) seems to be exemplary: it was composed with directly nationalist intentions, depicting village life with musical material transformed from popular and traditional sources by a contemporary, even advanced, compositional technique. The designs for the opera, as much as the music, are evidence of the same process of transformation at work. The stage sets of the 1882 production were of an idealised village, and the costumes a 'folk' dress.[36] (As a general rule, the idea of folk and national dress owes a great deal to costume designers in theatre and court spectacles. It may be significant that the only European nation without some concept of national and regional costume is England.) The wider search for the 'mother-tongue' included both the recovery of vanished (but real) pasts, the synthesis and transformation of still-existing peasant traditions (where they did exist), and the invention of traditions (where they did not).

33. Keseru, K. 'Vernacularism and its Special Characteristics in Hungarian Art', in Gordon-Bowe, N. (ed.) 1993, p. 129.

34. Gerle, J. 'What is Vernacular? The Search for the mother-Tongue of Forms', in Gordon-Bowe (ed.) op. cit., p. 144.

35. Ibid., pp. 145–6

36. See Illustrations in Large, B. *Smetana* (London, Duckworth 1970).

The invention of traditions has recently received a good deal of attention, but mainly within a framework of social history. I shall deal with this theme in more detail in the next chapter. For the moment, it is enough to point to the connections between these pseudo-traditions and the development of tourism, with the 'packaging' of local difference, and the complicity of the population in turning itself into a spectacle.[37]

37. See Brett, D. *On Decoration* (Cambridge, Lutterworth Press 1992) pp. 54–9, which I paraphrase here.

Within the British Isles, the assertion of national differences and distinct expressions led to some curious results, since real differences, insofar as they had ever existed coherently, had been severely eroded before the nineteenth century began. There was very little that could be distinguished as peasant art. Distinct expression had to be constructed, sometimes on the basis of very little evidence indeed. Nor was there a clearly defined 'Englishness' against which 'Irishness', 'Scottishness', etc. could measure themselves.

The fraudulent element in 'Highland culture' has been noticed above but where Ireland is concerned a different picture emerges, since the construction of difference was bound up with a partly successful political nationalism, and the existence of real objects and buildings that could with good reason be treated as authentically 'national'. The magnificent decorative art of ancient manuscripts, the metalwork, and the neat and chunky remains of Irish Romanesque churches were sufficiently unlike anything else to give the idea of a Celtic revival a basis in fact and scholarship. Carlyle, visiting the collection of the Royal Irish Academy in 1849, described it as a 'really interesting museum, for everything has a certain authenticity as well as national and other significance, too often wanting in such places'. Thus when W.H. Lynn designed the beautiful and meticulous neo-Romanesque Church of St Patrick, at Jordanstown near Belfast in 1867, he could reasonably claim it as 'the first attempt in modern times to revive the ancient architecture of Ireland'.

Architects like Lynn helped to set in motion a considerable and capable craft industry that produced some outstanding work. Inspired by arts and crafts values transposed from England to Irish themes, a number of organisations came into being with the aim – linked in varying degrees to political nationalism, and to different kinds of nationalism – of reviving 'traditional' Irish design. Jeanne Sheehy's recent study of the Celtic revival recounts attempts to invent a national costume, and she describes kilts, cloaks, brooches and the use of distinctive green tweed and yellow linen.[38]

38. See Sheehy, J. *The Rediscovery of Ireland's Past; the Celtic Revival 1830–1930* (London Thames and Hudson 1980), pp. 149–50 and also Larmour, P. *The Arts and Crafts Movement in Ireland* (Belfast, Friar's Bush Press 1992).

I have been describing, in an abbreviated form, some powerful reactions to the processes of primary industrialisation and the building of modern nations. These consisted in assertions of the pre-industrial past, and attempts to use versions of the past as templates

to change the course of the future. I write 'versions' of the past because no matter how scholarly, most are grounded in a retrospective utopianism; in many cases they are also grounded in an essentialist nationalism, seeking to recover the 'real' life of the people that modernity seems to have erased.

2.3 Church of St Patrick, Jordanstown, near Belfast. Designed by W.H. Lynn in 1867 as 'the first attempt in modern times to revive the ancient architecture of Ireland'.

But, clearly, there are significant differences between these different assertions and between different class and national experiences. The most brutal is the distinction between those who, with greater or lesser degrees of control or self-consciousness, are the agents of a process, and those who are the patients. When we turn from the formal culture and the world of rulers, owners and patrons to that of everyday life and popular experience (from the modernisers to those who were modernised), we begin to see the changes wrought by industrial production in a darker light. And one of the deep changes we see is in the sense of time.

Societies and eras differentiate between one another on the basis of their respective senses of time. The countryperson perceives the townsperson as frenetically hurried, whilst the townsperson groans with exasperation at country slowness. The extremes are met across major cultural divisions, between the tourist on schedule and the native life of (apparent) idleness. The servant demonstrates her power over the mistress by *making her wait*. One of the major markers of the threshold between peasant and industrial worker is the acquisition of a wristwatch. It takes no thought to see that these anecdotal examples have at their core an unequal relationship, in which different degrees or kinds of power encounter one another.

These differing senses of time are difficult to analyse directly, because they are existential and internalised; but they are not immune to investigation because they surface in customs and in cultural practices. As social behaviour changes (driven by material and other processes), so our account of time changes. The life of peasants is ordered around seasons and the tasks imposed by them; 'harvest-time' may be long or short, late or early, from one year to another; and counterpointed by festivals whose days are fixed. With greater division of labour, different time schemes develop, linked to different work rhythms. So the sailor's 'watch' is both a period of work and a group of people who work together. Thus it makes sense to speak of a change from 'peasant', or 'pre-industrial' time, to 'industrial' or 'modern' time and finally to much more general assumptions such as 'the increasing pace of modern life'. And if one grants a broad generality to these distinctions, they do not seem to be false. We can be confident that the clash between these imperfect periodisations and accurate 'timing' lies close to the heart of the retrospective impulse.

Though we cannot know with any certainty what pre-industrial time *felt* like, it was identified by the early theorists of mechanisation as inappropriate to industrial discipline; as part of a 'habitus' that had to be broken before industrialisation could reach its full achievement. Andrew Ure's *The Philosophy of Manufactures* (1835) is much concerned with this discipline. He describes the progressive invention of the modern factory in terms of automation and time-keeping habits.

> [E]very process, peculiarly nice, and therefore liable to injury from the ignorance and waywardness of workmen, is withdrawn from handicraft control and placed under the guidance of self-acting machinery . . . the main difficulty did not, in my apprehension, lie so much in the invention of a proper self-acting mechanism . . . as above all, in training human beings to renounce their desultory habits of work, and to identify themelves with the unvarying regularity of the complex automaton . . . Even at the present day, when the system is perfectly organized, and its labour lightened to the utmost, it is found nearly impossible to convert persons past the age of puberty, whether drawn from rural or from handicraft occupations, into useful factory hands. After struggling for a while to conquer their listless or restive habits, they either renounce the employment spontaneously, or are dismissed by the overlookers on account of inattention . . . By the infirmity of

human nature it happens, that the more skilful the workman, the more self-willed and intractable he is liable to become, and of course, the less fit a component of a mechanical system . . . The grand object therefore . . . is to reduce the task of workpeople to the exercise of vigilance and dexterity – faculties, when concentrated to one process, speedily brought to perfection in the young.[39]

Ure is one of those very few authors, like Machiavelli or von Clausewitz, who exposes the bare mechanics of power; the power described here is that of social transformation. The process requires the extirpation of habits and concepts of time so profound that it is best exercised upon unformed children. Desultory habits have to be replaced by unvarying regularity. In Bourdieu's terms, a new 'habitus' must be constructed.[40]

The distinction Ure makes is not sociological. It assumes the existence of unvarying and objective standards of measurement; that is to say it is informed by the physical sciences of the period, by Newtonian mechanics and the paramount necessity of accurate chronometry.[41] Such an account of time is at complete variance with time as individuals subjectively, and as pre-industrial societies collectively, imagine and mythologise it. The representation of the clash between the Enlightenment cosmos and the imaginative experience becomes, in due course, the major theme of romanticism at every level from the most sublime to the most mundane.

In William Blake's poems the collision and loss is clearly and consciously stated as a problem in the experience of time and workmanship. Blake was himself one of the army of the technologically unemployed.

> And all the arts of life they chang'd into the arts of death.
> The hour glass contemn'd because its simple workmanship
> Was as the workmanship of the plowman and the water wheel
> That raises water into Cisterns, broken and burned in fire
> Because its workmanship was like the workmanship of the shepherds
> And in their stead intricate wheels invented, Wheel without wheel
> To perplex youth in their outgoings and to bind to labours
> Of day and night the myriads of Eternity, that they might file
> and polish brass and iron hour after hour, laborious workmanship,
> Kept ignorant of the use   (*Jerusalem*)

At the humbler end of this scale we find the reflection of the weaver-poet who, forced to obtain work in a power-loom factory, lamented the effect of the change upon his verses:

> I then worked in a small chamber, overlooking Luddenden Churchyard. I used to go out in the fields and woods . . . at meal-times and listen to the songs of the summer birds, or watch the trembling

39. Ure, A. *The Philosophy of Manufactures* (London, C. Knight 1835), pp. 14–20. See also Brett 1984.

40. As a guide to historical reality, Ure's argument is altogether too abstract. The Lancashire cotton-mill was not the only site of industrial transformation, but only the most completely 'self-regulating'. Cotton spinners were widely recognised as the most wretched of the new factory operatives. In other areas of production the 'automatic system' took a much slower pace and was less drastically centralised. But that is not the point of his argument, which is addressed solely toward those bare mechanics of inequality and violent change.

41. The concept of an abstract and measurable time seems to have been both the effect and the cause of increasingly precise clock-design. The development of self-regulating machinery owes a great deal to the escapements, governors and leverage systems invented by the great chronometer-makers of the seventeenth century, and the association between time and space measurement for the purposes of navigation was one of the foundations of British naval supremacy – and hence scientific and industrial development. That the entire cosmos might be imagined as a vast clockwork of unvarying regularity (a master-image of Enlightenment) is of a piece with a culture that could arbitrarily decide to measure the universe from a redundant fortification in Greenwich.

42. Heaton, W. as quoted by E.P. Thompson in *The Making of the English Working Class* (London, V. Gollancz 1963), p. 294.

waters of the Luddon . . . But it is all over; I must continue to work amidst the clatter of machinery.[42]

What is described here, from within, from without, was seen as an unprecedented and threatening social upheaval. Around the same time a traveller (we might almost call him an industrial tourist) visited the astonishing new conurbations coming into being in the north of England, and wrote that

> As a stranger passes through the masses of human beings which have accumulated round the mills and print works . . . he cannot contemplate these 'crowded hives' without feelings of anxiety and apprehension almost amounting to dismay. The population, like the system to which it belongs, is NEW; but it is hourly increasing in breadth and strength. . . . The manufacturing population is not new in its formation alone: it is new in its habits of thought and action, which have been formed by the circumstances of its condition, with little instruction, and less guidance, from external sources.[43]

43. Cooke Taylor, W. *Notes of a Tour in the Manufacturing Districts of Lancashire* (1842) pp. 4–6 quoted by Thompson, op. cit., p. 190.

The Communist Manifesto (1848) remains the most vivid and often quoted statement of this experience:

> Constant revolutionizing of production, uninterrupted disturbance of all social relationships, everlasting uncertainty and agitation, distinguish the bourgeois epoch from all earlier times. All fixed, fast-frozen relationships, with their train of venerable ideas and opinions, are swept away, all new-formed ones become obsolete before they can ossify. All that is solid melts into air . . .

Under such conditions, time (in its concrete sense as social continuity) is 'speeded up' or seems to move in sudden 'jerks'. The sense of cause and effect 'in some sort of chronological sequence' becomes increasingly difficult to maintain without some very powerful and abstract theory (such as Marxism, to take the obvious example). Marx and Engels believed that the collapse and obsolescence of past and recent knowledge would mean that 'men are at last forced to face with sober sense the real conditions of their lives and their relations with their fellow men' (ibid.). But it may be that the extreme difficulty of negotiating rapid change, and the obstacles in the way of constructing an easily comprehended chronological sequence (which is another way of describing a popular history) actually dissolves the sense of there being real conditions that *can* be faced with sober rationality. Thus the world unrolls before us as a spectacle rather than as an arena for action.

Such historical changes, as is well recognised, produced a turbulent social and political atmosphere. Of the 1840s E.P. Thompson notes: 'It is, perhaps, the scale and intensity of this multiform popular agitation which has, more than anything else, given rise (among contemporary observers and historians alike) to a sense of *catastrophic* change.'[44]

44. Thompson op cit., p. 191.

Change on this scale, without the protection of wealth, is a process of immiseration. It strikes at our sense of continuous reality. The attempt to recover an imagined past, which would restore some sort of continuity, and reassert the former 'habitus', figured in many of these agitations, and from time to time made some headway in the world of action.

The Chartist Land Company identified machine production as the enemy of the people: 'It must be destroyed, or its injustice and inequality must be curbed by the possession of The Land' (*Northern Star*, 10 Jan. 1848). Only by independent possession of small holdings and by mixed occupation could a decent life be maintained in freedom. Feargus O'Connor's rhetoric stressed the vast improvement of life for women and children freed from the new work disciplines and 'the tyranny of the factory bell'. The company had as its aim the creation of small estates of small-holdings, and five such enterprises were begun before the scheme collapsed through O'Connor's idiosyncratic management and insufficient flow of funds.[45] O'Connor was criticised by other Chartist leaders for deflecting the political energies of the movement, but seen in retrospect we can identify his position as one which has had lasting consequences. The identical model cottages, built to a high standard, sturdy and functional, are the predecessors of many a rural development and council house, and they point a way forward toward 'garden city' theories.[46]

Many other examples might be cited here, though most fall under the heading of Utopian communities, Owenism and the communitarian movements that sought realisation in the New World. All were, in some measure, responses to a sense of catastrophic change and self-augmenting innovation: attempts at re-entry into vanished and imaginary circumstances.

We are not, of course, concerned here with the question as to whether or not the population was better fed and housed in 1850 than in 1800, nor with health statistics, mortality rates or legal status. Our concern is with how this change was represented to and by the population, in imagination, in commentary and in rhetoric. That is to say again that the study of representations is 'imaginative history' which brings with it the tropes, forms and patterns of association it has created in its past. Blake's lines link 'back' to chiliastic forebears, and 'sideways' to contemporary prophesies and to the taste for the sublime, through the use of characteristic rhythms and imagery. Just so, the weaver-poet reiterates a pastoral trope that is, as it were, 'hard-wired' into the possibilities of representation. These given forms re-appear in heritage rhetoric and spectacle today, because the process of capital and technology-driven change continues to produce uninterrupted disturbance of all social relationships, which demands an imaginative

45. This account is taken from Hadfield, A.M. *The Chartist Land Company* (London 1970).

46. How far O'Connor was drawing upon his personal Irish experience is not certain, but something of this rhetoric survived into the years of de Valera and the foundation of the Free State.

retrospection; and because that retrospection, *in the absence of critical reflection*, consists in the recreation of representations modelled upon other representations, in a 'precession' of imagery.

Most recent writers on the nature of modernity have concluded that it requires, or is implicated in, significant changes in our experience of both space and time. This is most clearly seen in the formal culture. The re-articulation of space is the common theme that links painting and architecture all through the major part of this century; a parallel exploration of time (or more precisely, continuity) links the philosophy of Bergson with the writings of Proust and Joyce. The development of film unified both pictorial space and narrative time in a single experience.

A smaller number of authors have identified a certain sense of time with what has been termed 'post-modernity'. Frederic Jameson, in particular, has described a contemporary reduction of experience as 'a series of pure and unrelated presents . . . a rush of filmic incidents without density'.[47] Robert Hewison, in his writings on heritage, has taken Jameson's argument further and asserts a definite linkage. 'Post-modernism and the heritage industry are linked . . . both conspire to create a shallow screen that intervenes between our present lives and our history.' This reduces history to 'a contemporary creation, more costume drama and re-enactment than critical discourse'.[48] These arguments, to which I shall return, are plausible, not least because they combine the visual with the temporal. As in spatial tourism we pass from one site to another, 'sight-seeing', taking away records in the form of photographs, so in the temporal tourism of a 'heritage centre' we pass from one epoch to another through series of simulations which are given verisimilitude by the employment of our other senses in an all-around spectacle. But Jameson goes on to argue that this is part of the entire cultural logic of late capitalism, which demands the commodification of everything; what he calls a 'contrived depthlessness'.

The difficulty with this approach to the problems posed by heritage is that these arguments depend very heavily upon contemporary theory and the culture in which it is embedded; but as I have shown, a great deal of what we would now term heritage began to take form in the early and mid-nineteenth century, in what I have loosely termed 'primary modernisation'; of this, contemporary theory has very little to say. Profound changes in our sense of time, and of cause and effect over time, well pre-date anything we might call 'post-modernity'. Furthermore, the argument of 'cultural logic' cannot but assume that its effects (being dependent upon 'late capitalism') are everywhere the same; but the existential facts of life, the local manifestations of culture, language and history, the particular economic pressures and so forth

47. Jameson, F. 'Postmodernism, or the Cultural Logic of Late Capitalism', *New Left Review*, 146 1984, p. 120.

48. Hewison, R. *The Heritage Industry* (London 1987), p. 135.

are always experienced locally, and inflect locally whatever is supposedly global. There are good reasons for refusing an easy explanatory status to the idea of 'late capitalism' (at least where heritage is concerned), because 'heritage' or heritage-like phenomena precede by many decades the present world-market system and 'post-Fordism'.

A more extreme case has been argued by Jean Baudrillard, who argues for a loss of 'the real' in an indefinite 'precession of simulacra' in which, as in a room full of mirrors, the image 'is never exchanged for the real, but exchanged for itself, in an uninterrupted circuit without reference or circumference'.[49] Ultimately, this founding of representation upon representation renders critical intervention impossible because:

> The impossibility of rediscovering an absolute level of the real is of the same order as the impossibility of staging illusion. Illusion is no longer possible, because the real is no longer possible. It is the *political* problem of parody, of hyperstimulation or offensive simulation, that is posed here.[50]

Such an argument leads us toward a mental landscape in which, since everything is pastiche, our own understandings are self-negating. This drops directly into an easy cultural pessimism. We might just as well give up thinking altogether and simply allow experience to wash over us in solipsistic passivity. Fortunately, the real keeps breaking in upon us with real hunger, real crimes, real ethical dilemmas, and even sometimes real joys. And if my main premise is correct, that heritage may be a contemporary form of popular history, then it becomes important to seek out those elements of thought that enable us build a positive criticism, which must be based on a sense of self and community that is neither contrived nor shallow. In a similar context, David Harvey has argued that:

> It is only in terms of such a centred sense of personal identity that individuals [*and societies*] can pursue objects over time, or think cogently about the production of a future significantly better than time present and time past.[51]

Such a position is grounded in a sense of the reality of history, of human beings as being historically created and self-creating. It is incompatible with traditional societies, insofar as (in the words of Mircea Eliade) traditional life means living 'in conformity with archetypes'[52] just as it is incompatible with the 'precession of simulacra'. The argument that I shall evolve during the conclusion of this study will include the proposition that 'heritage' is often part of an attempt to evade historical time and its real responsibilities, and to return us to a temporary condition of 'mythic' time/space, where there is relief

49. Baudrillard, J. (trans. Glaser) *Simulacra and Simulation* (Ann Arbor, Univ. of Michigan Press 1994), p. 6.

50. Ibid., p. 19.

51. Harvey (1989) op. cit., p. 53.

52. See Eliade, M. *The Myth of the Eternal Return, or Cosmos and History* (New York, Princeton UP, Bollingen Series 1954), p. 95.

from uninterrupted disturbance and everlasting uncertainty, and in which all that is solid does not melt into air.

Developing all through the nineteenth century, elements of what we would now call 'heritage' were part of a critical response to modernisation and industrial production. Very many more instances could be cited and analysed than there is space for here. Scholarly reconstruction, reverence for the past, a tautological concept of national culture, essentialist and de-historicised ideas of national character, elements of simulation and display were all present well before anything now called 'modernism' had come into being, let alone 'post-modernism'.

What prevents us from calling these elements 'heritage' is that they were conceived as programmes of action, as critical intentions, and that they had real effects in real worlds. That there were also fantastic and entertaining reconstructions, simulations and displays will be discussed in chapter 4, largely devoted to the technologies of representation.

It will also be clear that the account given above relates obliquely rather than directly to Irish experience. In seeking the nineteenth-century origins of the idea of 'heritage' and the attitudes and practices that are now associated with the idea, one needs to go to the fountainheads of primary industrial modernity. But we can indicate two experiences which accompanied the modernisation of Ireland, to which the 'catastrophic' theory certainly applies. The first was, clearly, famine, and the second, continually renewed in each generation, has been emigration. As Endre Ady wrote of his Hungarian countrymen – 'They left because it is impossible to live in this land unless every year a few hundred thousand human beings are exported.'[53]

Of the first, the cultural effects have been inconclusively studied, because the very topic is fraught with pseudo-histories and national mythologies. The view that I take of the matter (which is developed later in respect to the Strokestown Famine Museum) is 'anti-revisionist', not because of arguments about modernisation and the apportioning of blame, but because my concern is the history of representations, (and especially popular representations) and I know of no examples in which death by hunger was represented as anything other than catastrophic. That the Great Famine of the 1840s remains remarkably under-studied is itself an index of its apalling nature, and the difficulties involved in representing it. The problem is not unlike that presented one hundred years later by the Holocaust. As to the social consequences of the Famine, there is a consensus among historians that the terrible toll brought in its path a significant modernisation of land tenure, agriculture, social class structure and administration; that the Famine created a great caesura in Irish history.[54]

53. Ady, Endre 'Julian's Magyars', in *The Explosive Country* (Budapest, Corvina Books 1977), p. 105.

54. See Lee, J.J. *The Modernisation of Irish Society 1848–1918* (Dublin 1973); Whelan, K. 'The Famine and Post-Famine Adjustment', in Nolan, W. (ed.) *The Shaping of Ireland; The Geographical Perspective* (Dublin 1986) and Ó Gráda, C. *Ireland Before and After the Famine: Explorations in Economic History 1800–1925* (Manchester, Manchester University Press, 2nd edn., 1993).

Of the second, it is clear that Irish labour was essential for the English and Scots industrial revolution. Not simply because it was cheap but because, as a Birmingham employer witnessed, 'The Irish labourers will work any time . . . and Englishmen would not do the work they do'. By the late 1840s whole classes of menial work had passed almost entirely into the hands of immigrant labourers and their descendants.[55] Thus, with certain exceptions (notably in Belfast) the experience of primary modernisation was imported back into Ireland, and achieved by proxy. Within the ever wider diaspora of the later part of the century, the disconnection between the identity 'Irish' and the really existing country produced the now familiar demand for 'an imagined past'. This now appears as a global phenomenon:

> In a world with too many voices speaking all at once, a world where syncretism and parodic invention are becoming the rule, not the exception, an urban, multinational world of institutional transience – where American clothes made in Korea are worn by young people in Russia, where everyone's 'roots' are in some degree cut – in such a world it becomes increasingly difficult to attach human identity and meaning to a coherent 'culture' and 'language'.[56]

55. See Thompson op. cit., pp. 429–44 for discussion.

56. Clifford, J. *The Predicament of Culture: Twentieth-Century Literature and Art* (Harvard UP 1988), p. 95.

3

THE PICTURESQUE AND THE SUBLIME:
Toward the Aestheticisation of History

1. Benjamin, W. *Illuminations* (ed.) Arendt. (New York, Harcourt, Brace and World 1968), p. 243.

This chapter is concerned with the process whereby concepts formed for aesthetic and, more particularly, artistic purposes have been transferred from tourism and 'sight-seeing' to the presentation of the past. I shall call the final end of this process 'the aestheticisation of history', in order to recall Walter Benjamin's remarks on the aestheticisation of politics. 'The logical result of fascism,' he wrote, 'is the introduction of aesthetics into political life.'[1] The question that I would like to raise is something like the reverse query – namely, what is the logical result of the introduction of aesthetics into history?

We shall observe that, far from being 'immediate', the encounter with the past (constructed as 'heritage') is not only mediated by the obvious forms of museums, parks, exhibitions, reconstructions, etc., but has also undergone prior mediation through deeply rooted and almost invisible cultural assumptions and the languages of taste. Indeed, it is these assumptions and languages that may constitute the real substance of 'heritage'. As we have seen, these assumptions are embodied in literature, architecture and other cultural forms, not the least of which are the visual ideologies incorporated in painting and other systems of picture-making. It is to these that we now turn to investigate two terms with which we must engage – 'the picturesque' and 'the sublime'. It is under these headings, I shall argue, that the aestheticisation of history proceeds.

It is here that this study turns its attention directly to Irish examples, because Ireland, along with some other parts of Europe, is a *locus classicus* of sublimity and the picturesque. The idea of the sublime is, in its modern formulation, Ireland's most significant gift to the theory of taste, and the representation of Ireland to the world at large has been, and still is, through such terms; they have in some measure been adopted by the Irish themselves.

The process whereby a region or country is aestheticised is not, of course, an innocent process; it implies that the power of designation has passed from one nexus of command to another. The relationship between the tourist and the toured is always based upon what Edward

Said has called 'an uneven exchange'.[2] Typically, a 'peripheral' area or country is designated as picturesque or sublime by visitors from a metropolitan 'centre', to whom the local inhabitants are economically and politically subordinate; the locals then take on, with greater or lesser degrees of complicity, aspects of the roles assigned them in order to profit from the visitors. A cursory look at the literature and imagery of Bord Fáilte will see this process at work. (This is the process which McCandless designates as 'staged authenticity'.) However, we shall also see how 'peripheral' countries and communities can come to see themselves as picturesque and, as it were, internalise the values of the 'centre', and how an imagery created 'for-others' can coincide with that created 'for-self', and how this imagery can have real-life consequences in the form of government policy and ideology.

2. Said, E. *Orientalism* (1978), p. 12.

As Malcolm Chapman argues, centres and peripheries are not fixed places, but directions in which fashions and concepts migrate. The 'periphery' itself – always looking 'centrally' – abandons fashions and concepts to its own periphery so that finally they come to rest at 'the edge'. Here fashions and concepts come to die; to abandon them is final. 'It is easy to see, then, how fringe dwellers come to be seen as occupants of history, guardians of tradition, and so forth, with moral responsibility for the preservation of heritage.'[3] While this argument has the merit of explaining how some people, including the Irish (and *a fortiori* the most westerly Irish), come to be seen as romantically interesting, picturesque and sublime by metropolitan standards, it does not, I think, add to our understanding of contemporary conditions in which, over large fields of human communication, geographical distance is of no significance at all. However, that is a matter to which we will return later in this study.

3. There are valuable discussions of this problem in Chapman (1992), see esp. pp. 95–8.

A short study of the implications of 'the picturesque' and 'the sublime' establishes some criteria that underlie the aestheticisation of history. This cannot, of course, engage with the full implications of picturesque-ness and sublimity; it treats of them as elements in the history of representations, which are essential for a full understanding of the heritage concept and its power. With their help, and with a further consideration of the technologies of their representation, we can begin to develop a critical method by which heritage sites (museums, parks, centres, etc.) can be analysed and assessed.

The Picturesque

In 1753 Mrs Elizabeth Montagu, a lady of strong intellectual and artistic tastes, wrote to a friend to describe a picnic near Tunbridge Wells, in Kent:

4. Letters (1813) Vol. 3. pp. 235–6 quoted in Andrews, M. *The Search for the Picturesque* (Stanford UP 1989), p. 39. In what follows below I am generally indebted to Andrews. And see also *The Genius of the Place; The English Landscape Garden 1620–1820*, J. Dixon Hunt and P. Willis (eds.), (London, Paul Elek 1975) for a remarkable collection of documents.

5. Lynd, R. *Home Life in Ireland* (London, Mills and Boone 1912), p. 29.

6. Detailed critiques of the concept of 'the aesthetic experience' have been undertaken by Pierre Bourdieu in *Distinctions: a Social Critique of the Judgement of Taste* (Cambridge Mass., Harvard University Press 1984), and Terry Eagleton in *The Ideology of the Aesthetic* (Oxford, Basil Blackwell 1990), from sociological and neo-Marxist perspectives. While this study shares much of those critiques, I would maintain that neither deal adequately with the actual experience that we have when we encounter something that seems to us beautiful or apt, nor with the experience of finding new beauty. That is to say that one can't reduce the 'aesthetic experience' to ideology; though the organisation of beauty and pleasure into taste (as in the picturesque) is certainly part of a visual ideology.

7. See Hadjinicolaou, op. cit., ch. 13 for a distinction between 'positive' and 'critical' visual ideology. 'Every collective visual ideology is positive. This derives from the fact that, being in origin necessarily the visual ideology of a single social class or section of a class, it represents the way in which that class sees itself and the world. A class can only see itself and the world positively; that is to say, it defines itself in relation to, and by means of, the "values" which belong to it.' However, individual pictures may manifest a critical position.

Mr Pitt . . . ordered a tent to be pitched, tea to be prepared, and his French horn to breath Music like the unseen Genius of the woods . . . After tea we rambled about for an hour, seeing several views, some wild as Salvator Rosa, others placid, and with the setting sun, worthy of Claude Lorrain.[4]

One hundred and fifty-nine years later Robert Lynd, travel writer and enthusiast for Achill Island, wrote of an evening walk that:

Out in the darkness you see the women labouring and bringing wonder into the rocky darkness of the island with their heavy petticoats of red and blue that you will not surpass for colour in a Titian.[5]

The movement of taste that we call, loosely, 'the picturesque' has as its aim the validation of experience by art. Certain kinds of scenery, certain buildings, human figures in landscape, are valued according to their prior appearance in painting. This reverses the ancient (and indeed, 'common-sense') principle whereby art is validated by matching it against nature and experience.

The term 'picturesque' was originally derived from the Italian *pittoresco*, which had no special reference to landscape, but was addressed to any subject thought to be paintable. William Gilpin in his 'Essay on Prints' (1768) defined it as 'that kind of beauty which would look well in a picture'. The exact stages by which, in the course of the eighteenth century, this term was elevated into a principle of educated taste are not our concern here; but several features of the matured concept of 'the picturesque' have a direct bearing on our topic, through the growth of tourism, and then through the application of its principles to reconstructions of the past.

The first of these is that of unequal power. To be able to view a tract of countryside (that is, an arena for effort) or a scene of women at work *as if it were a painting* is to take up a privileged position of detachment and disinterest.[6] Those who work the land very rarely regard it as art. And those who live in sublime landscapes frequently regard them as dreary wilderness from which they long to escape.

In the eighteenth century the privileged position was embedded in social class and education to a very marked degree. To perceive the landscape as a *pastorale* was only possible to one versed either directly in a classical education, reading Virgil and Horace without self-consciousness, or taking in Augustan attitudes through translation or paraphrase. This perception was an important part of the 'positive visual ideology' by which the wealthy and powerful understood and validated their existence.[7] In its most privileged instances, the perception of the landscape turned from passive to active, and land was remodelled to accord with artistic principles. It is well recognised that there are many links between the notion of the picturesque and the development of country estates and other real environments by landscaping, planting and gardening, which in turn are reflected in contemporary ideas of 'authentic' and 'traditional' landscape.

But as the years move on, this privileged position becomes both more generally available and less permanent. Mrs Montague's picnic, complete with tent, musicians and servants, was evidently a grand affair; but by the time we reach 1912, Robert Lynd's readers were no more than averagely well-off middle-class tourists who travelled by rail (or possibly motor car), and could afford to stay in hotels. Lynd assumes that they have a visual education, but most likely from illustrated books or from visiting the National Gallery in London. They would have been aware, too, of attempts to create a national collection for Ireland, and to found an 'Irish School' of painting. Today's tourist in Ireland is unlikely to be privileged in any formal or permanent sense (within European terms), but is able to take up the position of privilege, as a spectator of the scene and as a brief participant in a situation of leisure (replete with unusual accomodation, a service industry, and 'traditional' music provided as appropriate).

We shall return to this concept of privilege on several occasions because the essence of the pleasures of privilege is irresponsibility. The aesthetic position implied in the picturesque denies its own problems. The eighteenth-century landowner 'improving' his estate according to picturesque principles may or may not have had the welfare of the tenants in mind (and often did), but it could only be incidentally or the principles would not have been picturesque. As Robert Lynd was describing Achill, the island was the scene of sporadic lawlessness and chronic poverty, relieved only by seasonal emigration. Lynd, as a nationalist and a member of Sinn Féin, was well aware of this, but was unable to bring that understanding into the conventions of picturesque travel-writing because the one would annihilate the other. And today's visitor to the 'stately home' generally sees only the results of an historic process, not the process itself, with its horrors and triumphs.

Secondly, as a specifically artistic concept, the picturesque is the origin of several practices that we now see to be typical of tourism. Though they do not always relate directly to heritage, they are part of the full set of activities that impinge upon our topic.

First among these practices is the pursuit of particular kinds of scenes and subjects. It was through picturesque subjects that rural life was re-imagined for city dwellers and the idea of national scenery was conceived. Joseph Warton, writing in 1756, noted that 'It is only within a few years that the picturesque scenes of our own country, lakes, mountains, cascades, caverns and castles, have been visited and

8. Warton, Joseph *An Essay on the Genius and Writings of Pope* 1756, 4th edn. 1782. II p. 185. quoted by Andrews, op. cit.

9. Gilpin, William *Observations Relative Chiefly to Picturesque Beauty etc.* (1786) vol. 2 p. 44, cited by Andrews, ibid.

described.'[8] With the lakes and mountains and castles went appropriate persons, largely representing the virtues of country simplicity or honest labour. Human figures were, however, quite definitely subordinate to the harmony of a nature that was humanised by signs of habitation and history, without being extensively peopled. There was also a counter-position which claimed that 'in a moral view, the industrious mechanic is a more pleasing object than the loitering peasant. But in a picturesque light, it is otherwise'.[9] Ireland, and particularly its western parts, was such an area; well provided with lakes, mountains, ruins and peasants both labouring and loitering.

Not all scenes were, of course, picturesque. A judicious blending of nature and art was required. Ruins were admired because they showed the modification of the one by the other. Ireland was specially rich in ruins; William Gilpin referred to Oliver Cromwell as 'that picturesque genius [who] omitted no opportunity of adorning the countries through which he passed, with noble ruins'. Wild scenery, that could not be 'improved' and did not show the hand of man, was usually thought too savage (though the concept of the sublime enabled wildness to be incorporated into the picturesque). But a wild scene could be humanised by a carefully located cottage. Distant prospects were admired, and the choice of viewpoints was always considered very carefully.

With this subject matter went a demand for certain kinds of composition and tonal values, which included varied handling of paint, deep recessional space, particular balances of foreground, middle ground and background (rather in the manner of theatre scene painting), and carefully unified tones. In the next chapter I shall return to the importance of theatrical scene painting and its conventions.

The use of watercolour gained a particular importance in the process whereby these strictly painterly values came to the fore; within the purview of picturesque taste, a washed drawing could have as much prestige as any other medium, since it was direct and less mediated by studio traditions and therefore more 'natural' and 'spontaneous'.

As an aid to identifying and capturing appropriate scenes, a number of viewing devices were created. The most striking of these was the 'Claude Glass'. This was an arrangement of convex mirror and darkened glass, whereby an image was reflected down onto a screen and shown there with tones suitably harmonised and unified, in the approved taste. The device was normally folded away in the pocket, not unlike a cigarette case or powder compact, and was brought out in order to test real scenes for their picturesque qualities. Other simpler devices were frames that could be held up, to 'frame' the landscape, just as photographers and cameramen today hold up both hands to 'frame' a 'shot' between fingers and thumbs.

The Claude Glass in its turn was descended from the various forms of *camera obscura* and *camera lucida*, and the perspectival devices that painters had used for two centuries and longer. It was used in conjunction with the sketchbook, pencil and wash to make rapid notational drawings as an aid to studio work, or as a means to find out suitable compositions in nature. Thus the Claude Glass was part of the prehistory of the camera, and it is useful in this connection to see the early camera as a combination of glass-and-sketchpad. Some glasses produced an image with similar size and proportions to the modern postcard.

If one was not a painter, but a lady or gentleman travelling for pleasure ('making a tour'), the Claude Glass was also a means of entering into the world of the painter – that is, self-validating your activity. There are accounts of travellers viewing the passing scene through their glass from the windows of a coach:

> A succession of high-coloured pictures is continually gliding before the eye. They are like the visions of the imagination; or the brilliant land-scapes of a dream. Forms, and colours, in brightest array, fleet before us; and if the transient glance of a good composition happen to unite with them, we would give any price to fix, and appropriate the scene.[10]

The language of this and other like passages is extremely suggestive of what was to follow; we have here the embryo form of Jameson's 'contrived depthlessness', 'the series of pure and unrelated presents . . . filmic incidents without density', and even Hewison's 'shallow screen that intervenes'. The reader will note the photo-chemical associations of 'to fix', and the commodity implications of 'appropriating the scene'. (In passing, we note that the whole language of photography, which largely derives from that of the picturesque, contains a scarcely veiled imagery of hunting and shooting. Shooting, taking, fixing, loading, etc. are among the central verb-phrases of the activity, and it is as if the photographer, like the picturesque artist before, were a hunter of scenes who captured them to bring them back as trophies, like the heads of elks and elephants.)

In the third place, the pursuit of the picturesque by both painter and connoisseur led directly to modern tourism. The most significant date by which to mark its inception might be 1782, with the publication of William Gilpin's *Observations on the River Wye, and Several Parts of South Wales etc., relative chiefly to Picturesque Beauty*. The manuscript had been circulating for twelve years before publication, which had been delayed because Gilpin could find no process capable of reproducing the pen-and-wash drawings by which it was illustrated. By the mid-1770s however, the use of aquatint had made adequate printing possible; this is a very early

10. Gilpin, *Remarks on Forest Scenery etc.* (1791), vol. 1, p. 225, cited by Andrews, ibid.

example of the importance of image reproduction in the fostering of tourism.

The book describes a journey by boat down the Wye valley for the purposes of admiring and painting the scenery. This was not a new activity, but Gilpin's text and illustrations made it popular. The book ran to its fifth edition before the end of the century, and was joined by other works: on *The Mountains, and Lakes of Cumberland and Westmoreland* (1786), on the *High-Lands of Scotland* (1789), *On Forest Scenery* (1791) and others. By the end of the century at least eight pleasure boats, equipped with awnings and drawing tables, were carrying tourists up and down the River Wye during the summer months. Subsequent writers enlarged upon Gilpin's themes and topics, and numerous other guidebooks appeared, both for the Wye and for the other picturesque regions.

However, for those less leisured, an alternative was soon to be available. By the 1790s (as we shall see in the next chapter) optical instruments were being used to create vast 360° 'panoramas' that took the picturesque view to gigantic proportions with the aid of theatrical scene-painters, architects and showpeople – and brought it to town. It thus became possible to take a picturesque tour without ever leaving the city; a form of vicarious tourism or 'pictorial conveyance'.

However, an important part of the actual tour was the sense of adventure involved and the chance to visit unusually wild or difficult places. North Wales was particularly favoured. Here was the combination of picturesque detail with sublime roughness and magnificence. The first truly picturesque tour of the principality seems to have been in 1771, when Sir Watkin Williams-Wynn made an extensive tour of the north, taking with him the artist Paul Sandby, whose watercolours were later printed in aquatint as *Twelve Views in North Wales* (1776). Thomas Pennant's *Tour in Wales* (1778–81) established the region as a venue for tourists, and though the author was not much concerned with artistic values, those that followed him were often artists or patrons of artists. In addition to Sandby, Richard Wilson, Thomas Rowlandson, and J.M.W. Turner and many lesser figures all made paintings and drawings of the established sites. North Wales was also perceived to be highly 'sublime' by virtue of its bardic and ancient Celtic associations.

Here the picturesque and the invented tradition could coincide. It was a period in which 'Welsh scholars and patriots rediscovered the past, historical, linguistic and literary traditions, and where those traditions were inadequate, they created a past which had never existed'.[11] This is a complicated story, in which the most serious scholarship was shot through with fraudulence and self-deception on

11. Morgan, P. 'From a Death to a View: the Hunt for the Welsh Past in the Romantic Period', in Hobsbawn and Ranger, (eds.) (1983), p. 43.

a grand scale; but it has been summarised as 'the rediscovery of the Celts'.[12] Much of this turned on an investigation of the origins of the Welsh language and its connections with Breton, Cornish, and Irish and Scots Gaelic, and the postulate of a grandiose Celtic history.[13]

The English Lake District was, as is well recognised, another prime site of the picturesque. As Andrews observes: 'From the 1770s onward, the lake scenery of Cumberland and Westmoreland was a serious challenge to the aesthetic supremacy of the European Grand Tour.'[14] Here the first important guidebook was Thomas West's *Guide to the Lakes* (1778), which went through several editions and rewritings in the next few years. As before it was addressed mainly to painters, designating particular sites as 'stations' from which the most picturesque views could be painted or visited. Greatly admired were the mirror-like qualities of each lake, which, like a vast Claude Glass, harmonised the nature around it by unifying the visual tonality. Language and attitudes developed here were later transferred to Irish locations such as Killarney and Connemara, not least the erotic transformation of 'female natives'.

> in this sequestered vale we met with a female native of youth, innocence and beauty; simplicity adorned her looks with modesty, and hid her down-cast eye; virgin apprehension covered her with blushes . . . her eyes . . . her lips . . . and on her full forehead ringlets of auburn flowed carelessly: a delicacy of proportion was seen over her whole figure, which was easy and elegant as nature's self.[15]

Such meetings were given formally poetic description by Wordsworth in his lines 'To a Highland Girl':

> . . . a very shower
> of beauty is thy earthly dower.
> Thou wear'st upon thy forehead clear
> The freedom of a mountaineer.
> (*Works*, p. 228)

Passages such as this look back to Rousseau (*Emile* published in 1762) and forward to Paul Gauguin's paintings of Tahitian beauties. It continues in travel-writing, and we are not surprised to find H.V. Morton, as late as 1930, meeting a bare-legged girl in Connemara.

> I would not call her beautiful, but she was sensational in her complete unconsciousness of sex. Here, within twenty-four hours of London, was a primitive woman . . . she did not know that she was cast in the same mould as Helen of Troy.[16]

We can discern all through the later nineteenth century a tendency to describe the 'Celtic' in feminine terms.[17] Here the land

12. Ibid., pp. 67–74. And see also 'Celticism and the Annulment of History' by George Watson in *Irish Studies*, 9, Winter 1994/5, pp. 2–6. He described Celticism as 'a system of representation imposed by a hegemonic group on others with such success that those others begin to accept the truth of that alien representation . . . a construction of urban intellectuals imposed on the predominantly rural denizens of what has come to be called the "Celtic fringe". . .' And, *a fortiori*, Chapman (1992) argues that it is not so much the rediscovery of the Celts, but their construction.

13. See particularly Chapman (1992).

14. Andrews, op. cit., p. 153.

15. Ibid., p. 175.

16. Morton, H.V. *In Search of Ireland* (London, Methuen 6th. edn. 1932), pp. 185–9. And see also Nash, C. 'The West of Ireland and Irish Identity', in O'Connor and Cronin, (eds.) (1993) for a discussion of 'the visitor's gaze and the landscape of desire'.

17. See for example Matthew Arnold *The Study of Celtic Literature* (London, Smith and Elder 1867), many refs.

(personified as a woman) is viewed *as if it were feminine*, and vice versa. The consequences of this need to be investigated in the light of recent feminist theory. As Chapman points out,

> [I]t is . . . the product of the similar structural positions which men occupy in relation to women, and which the centre occupies in relation to the social periphery – and in both cases, the relationship is one between 'definer' and 'defined'.[18]

18. Chapman, op. cit., pp. 216–17.

Viewed in these terms, the picturesque is a means of 'gendering' the landscape.

In Scotland the cult of the picturesque was mingled with 'sublimity'. It was hardly possible to see the Highlands as a place for pastoral improvement, and the terrible and the heroic were not emotions natural to the cult. Instead, the landscape was seen increasingly (as in north Wales) as a stage-setting for romantic epic. As one traveller wrote, entering the Highlands:

> I began to reflect that I was entering the land of Ossian's heroes; the land which presented those few simple, grand and gloomy objects which gave a melancholy cast to the imagination of the poet, and supplied that sublime, but undiversified imagery which forms one of the most peculiar characteristics of ancient Gaelic poetry.[19]

19. Robert Heron *Observations made in a Journey through the Western Counties of Scotland in 1792* (Perth 1793), quoted by Andrews, op. cit., p. 213.

The picturesque tour was facilitated by improved roads, those in the Highlands owing much to military engineers. In Ireland, travel remained difficult for longer, but when it became easier, in the early part of the next century, then Ireland too became open for aesthetic investigation and touring. Following picturesque precepts, only certain regions were favoured; particularly the West. Co. Clare became a centre for visitors drawn both to scenery and sea-bathing. Since continental Europe was closed to tourism, the first ten years of the nineteenth century saw a rapid development of hotels and other accommodation in villages like Kilkee.[20]

20. See Heuston, J. 'Kilkee – the Origins and Development of West Coast resort', in O'Connor and Cronin (eds.) (1993).

A characteristic product of this period (the 1840s) is the long series of paintings by W.H. Bartlett, subsequently engraved by R. Branchard and hand tinted, which take the viewer on a journey all around Ireland. A fine example is seen in his image of Fair Head (1845) in which two foreground figures contemplate (from a risky position) the tremendous middle-ground cliffs and the far-ground vistas of Antrim. The inability of this pictorial convention to deal with the real condition of the real inhabitants (then entering upon the Great Famine) is touched upon in chapter 5 below.

Concurrently, a small literature came into being that extolled Connemara to the hunter, the fisherman and the artist – three activities all formative of tourism and linked by the pursuit of the wild.

The artist by whom this district has not been visited, can indeed
have no idea of its surpassing grandeur and sublimity; go where he
will, he finds a picture . . . add to this that every peasant the artist
will encounter furnishes a striking and picturesque sketch, and as
they are usually met in groups, scarcely one will be without this
valuable accessory to the landscape.[21]

21. Hall and Hall, S. *Ireland,
its Scenery and Character*
(London, Howe 1841).

Connemara was an area where, according to the 1877 edition of
the Midland Great Western Railway tourist handbook, the tourist
'can visit a succession of really interesting and picturesque spots,
from which a vast variety of charming and memorable excursions
can be made . . . many and powerful fascinations . . . meet the eye
at every step'. The most significant of the artists who made their way
to the west was Robert Lynd's friend Paul Henry, whose paintings
were in time taken up by the railway company and turned into
posters. This imagery then returns to literature through another
generation of writers, such as H.V. Morton, already mentioned,
whose *In Search of Ireland* (1930) reads at times like a Henry
painting:

> It is a grey land, and the golden clouds ride up over the edge of
> it . . . the white road twists like a snake between the grey walls and
> over it walk strong bare-legged girls, wearing scarlet skirts and
> Titian-blue aprons. They swing from the hips as they walk with the
> grace of those who have never known shoe-leather.[22]

22. Morton op. cit., p. 172.

Contemporary critics saw Henry's paintings in terms of a Celtic
'essence', a 'common race instinct' which found expression in a
poetic and idealised approach to nature. This notion, that had
lately been expressed by Ernest Renan in his *The Poetry of the Celtic
Races* was perhaps a late outcome of the Ossianic enthusiasm of a
hundred years before.[23] The Exhibition of Irish Art held at the
Guildhall, London during 1904 had a special landscape section
containing over thirty scenes of Ireland, Brittany and Wales.[24]

23. Renan's book was first
published in French in
1854. I am indebted here
to unpublished research by
Mary Cosgrove, and see
also Chapman, p. 215.

   Viewed in this way, we can see the picturesque as the means by
which the idea of national and regional landscape was defined, first as
an idea and then as a stereotype. In the particular case of Ireland, this
process centred upon Connacht; both as viewed from without
Ireland, as well as from within. Some of the steps of this construction
have been studied by Catherine Nash[25] but for my purposes in this
chapter I am more concerned with the wider treatment of the 'Celtic
fringe' in relation to the concept of sublimity (*see* below).

24. Lane, Hugh
'Introduction' to the
1904 Exhibition, The
Guildhall, London. p. x.

25. op. cit.

   By the later nineteenth century, the picturesque had become a
very wide and general term again, covering for artistic purposes all
sorts of genre scenes, rural and domestic subjects and art practices.
The most influential writing on drawing, John Ruskin's *The Elements*

26. See Brett (1992b), pp. 24–6 and other writings.

of Drawing (first edn. 1857), is thoroughly permeated with picturesque language.[26] Ruskin's stress upon tonal values, upon what was termed 'natural facts' and upon the handling of the media of drawing, are all rooted in picturesque theory. But by 1857 this theory had acquired a different ideological force. In Ruskin's argument it becomes part of the defence of 'historical association' against contemporary science and industry. Picturesque values are re-asserted in architecture through the arts and crafts movements (as we have noted in chapter 2) and transmitted through to today by concepts of 'traditional design', 'the country garden', and (of course) a range of tourist publications. Luke Gibbons has suggested that

> [T]he absence of a visual tradition in Ireland, equal in stature to its powerful literary counterpart, has meant that the dominant images of Ireland have, for the most part, emanated from outside the country, or have been produced at home with an eye on the foreign (or tourist) market.[27]

27. See Gibbons, L. 'Alien Eye: Photography and Ireland', *CIRCA*, 12, p. 10; and also O'Connor, B. (1993)

Denis Donohue has also observed that

> Perched on the periphery of Europe [the Irish] have long been accustomed to the sense that our destinies and our very descriptions are forged by persons of superior power elsewhere.[28]

28. O'Connor (1993), p. 70.

However, a study of the picturesque tradition, as it has worked on the representation of Ireland, seriously qualifies this assertion, because whether 'home' or 'foreign', the aestheticisation process is always *de haut en bas;* and a good deal of Irish imagery (notably, that of Paul Henry, Grace Henry and their colleagues) was created as part of a putative 'Irish School', toward a nationalist cultural programme. Thus we can see the work of the Henrys, and several other artists, as creating within Ireland and for Ireland, a picturesque special domain that is both politically 'at home', but also a primitive 'Other' that nevertheless symbolises the nation as a whole. National stereotypes are as much the creation of nationalists as of visitors; within the field of Irish painting, as much as in some Irish writing, the relationships between landscape, human life and climate is a mirror image of 'colonialist' attitudes. Indeed, there is an argument to be made that the aesthetic values of the picturesque were internalised by Irish nationalism, which then projected them as ruralist policies during the Free State period.

In fact, what may be said about Ireland's picturesque 'national image' can be said about numerous 'regional images', of which the English Lake District stands as a typical example. Though the district was identified as a picturesque site by the first artist/tourists, their imagery and conceptual schema were given definitive form by a locally born poet and by local hoteliers. To designate oneself as picturesque and to enter into complicity with metropolitan expectations is a kind of knowing self-marginalisation which is, viewed in the light of Rousseau, a re-centring of the world upon the rural and the picturesque in such a way as to designate the metropolis as the divergent and abnormal – as part of metropolitan taste.

The remaining central feature of the picturesque which we have to consider is the extension of its principles from the observation of landscape to the creation of landscape. The title page of Uvedale Price's *Essays on the Picturesque* (1794) states the main theme in the subtitle – 'on the Use of Studying Pictures for the Purpose of improving Real Landscape'.[29] It is not my intention to engage with the traditions of landscape design, though reference will be made to them later in this study. What is of importance, and deserving of much closer study, is the continuance of the picturesque in concepts such as 'national heritage', 'national parks', councils for the preservation of rural scenes, and their embodiment in planning legislation that lend institutional force to Ruskinian sentiment. We can also see it at work in specific cases of 'heritage environment'.

These general issues of landscape and its meaning have been raised recently, in an Irish context, by John Feehan, who writes of 'the need for a blossoming of community awareness of the nature and importance of landscape heritage' and the 'enrichment of local community understanding of landscape heritage'. He and his colleagues in the rural tourism movement are much concerned with the management of countryside, and the development of a sympathetic and sustainable 'tourism on the farm'.[30] They see the Irish landscape as a collective artefact, established over five thousand years of settlement.

Now in this they are surely correct; what we see in land (at any level above the geological) is largely what we have made of it. It is, amongst other things, an artefact produced by concepts of ownership, rights and tenantry, as well as the product of methods of agriculture and of the exploitation of natural resources. It is therefore the product of systems of power (in the Irish example, notoriously so). But through adopting aesthetic criteria based upon the picturesque, they are led into the problematic assertion of an 'authentic' landscape. In a similar context, Patrick Duffy writes:

> Because the Irish agricultural economy has been relatively undeveloped for so long, landscape and settlement has been comparatively unchanged in a European context. Unlike, for example, the Netherlands and S.E. England, much of the Irish landscape is untouched, and remains today one of the most authentic countrysides in Europe.[31]

29. The full title is '*Essays on the Picturesque as Compared with the Sublime and the Beautiful, and on the Use of Studying Pictures for the Purpose of improving Real Landscape* (London, J. Mawman 1810 edn., 3 vols).

30. See Feehan, J. 'Farm Tourism', in *Heritage and Tourism; Second Conference on the Development of Heritage Attractions in Ireland* (Dublin, Bord Fáilte 1992), pp. 1–2 and *Tourism on the Farm* (Environmental Institute, University College, Dublin 1992). I should add that I feel a strong sympathy for the guiding ideas expressed in these publications, but also a need to rescue them from the tendencies of their own ideology!

31. Duffy, P.J. 'Conflicts in Tourism and Heritage', *The Newsletter of the Study of Irish Historic Settlement*, 1, Spring 1993.

3.1 Vignette by Michael Viney from *Tourism on the Farm*, John Feehan (ed.) (1992).

The oddness of this concept is revealed if we reverse it and ask ourselves what might be meant by an 'inauthentic' countryside?

With cultural expectations formed by the picturesque we delight in the small field patterns, the poor quality of drainage, the amount of waste ground, etc. That is to say, we are actually de-historicising the countryside from a place created by real human agencies, to an object of aesthetic contemplation, and failing to see it as a location for productive work. Considered from the point of vantage I am seeking to establish, of the 'imaginative history' of representations and 'heritage' as a form of popular history, the writings on 'farm tourism' and their choice of illustrations are straight within the picturesque tradition.

It might prove more useful to revise the idea of 'authentic landscape' and 'landscape heritage' in the light of the notion of 'vernacular landscape' – that which is the product of its immediate inhabitants and their forebears. This enables us to perceive and study landscape as a genuinely historical topic – subject to real economic, technological, proprietorial and other forces.[32] In this sense, the modern Irish landscape is, on the whole, vernacular and formed by small-scale farming which we can (with some reservation) describe as 'traditional'. But that again would be to project one aesthetic convention onto another, because that 'traditional' means, in historical fact, post-Famine. Pre-Famine field patterns were an unsupportable mix of 'rundale' communal allotments (of an improvised and subsistence character), large estates and an increasing number of small tenant farms. The effect of famine was to destroy the rundale system and consolidate the small farms, with their distinctive field patterns.[33] Subsequently, large estates were broken up or made over into secure tenantries, with the same effect. More recently large-scale and capital-intensive operations have come into being, not least in the industrialisation of turf-digging and the onset of 'agribusiness'; these operations are clearly not 'vernacular', but they have their own authenticity.

If we look at concepts of taste with a view to their historicity, and the functions they have served, we are compelled to think critically and to admit of multiple interpretive strategies. And it is through the multiplicity of conflicting interpretations that a history is formed. In Ireland, as we shall see, the meeting of the picturesque with the sublime has been and continues to be part of the construction of the 'Irish nation'.

The Sublime

The concept of the sublime, which partly overlaps and qualifies that of the picturesque, is also contributory to the aestheticisation of history. By presenting the past as mysterious and awesome, human actions are made to seem part of 'nature' (i.e. beyond question). Sublime objects or actions are beyond question because, as Burke observes, they cause 'astonishment'. 'In this case the mind is so entirely filled with its object, that it cannot entertain any other, nor by consequence reason on that object which employs it.'[34] Allied to astonishment is 'terror' and 'obscurity'.

32. See for example Jackson, J.B. *Discovering the Vernacular Landscape* (Yale UP 1984).

33. See Whelan, K. 'Pre and post-Famine Landscape Change', in Portéir, C. (ed.) *The Great Irish Famine: The Thomas Davis Lecture Series* (Dublin, RTÉ/Mercier Press 1995), pp. 19–33. To make matters more complicated, the immediate pre-Famine landscape was itself a product of an imbalance between pasturage and tillage and a 'population explosion'; and, Whelan argues, the rundale system acted as a 'mobile pioneering fringe' extending settlement over previously uncultivated uplands and boglands; in the process, destroying hitherto 'traditional' patterns.

34. Burke (1757), pt 2, p. 1.

3.2 W. H. Bartlett: Fairhead 1845. The picturesque meets the sublime on the 'Celtic Fringe'.

35. Ibid., pt 2, p. 4.

36. Ibid., pt 2, p. 10.

37. Kant, Immanuel *Crit. of Judgement* 28.11, trans. Meredith (Oxford 1952 edn.)

In nature dark, confused, uncertain images have a greater power on the fancy to form the grander passions than those which are more clear and determinate . . . hardly anything can strike the mind with its greatness, which does not make some sort of approach towards infinity.[35]

Vast size is also 'a powerful cause of the sublime', and where buildings are concerned, repetition and uniformity: 'There is nothing more prejudicial to the grandeur of buildings than . . . [writes Burke] . . . an inordinate thirst for variety.'[36]

As subsequently developed by Kant in the *Critique of Judgement* (1790), the sublime is given a humanising role, because it reveals our difference from nature. A key passage would be the following:

The irresistibility of the might of nature forces upon us the recognition of our physical helplessness as beings of nature, but at the same time reveals a faculty of estimating ourselves as independent of nature, and discovers a pre-eminence above nature that is the foundation of a self-preservation of quite another kind.[37]

The sublime, Kant argues, raises the imagination to that point at which 'the mind can make itself sensible of the appropriate sublimity of the sphere of its own being, even above nature'. In this aspect, of overwhelming power being itself transcended, the sublime is the lynchpin of romanticism and, some have argued, the founding moment of an important aspect of modernism.

A life attuned to the grandeur of nature attains its own sublimity; thus the savage past of epic and the extravagant future of science fiction are both expressions of the sublime: or, more accurately, attempts to imagine what such an attunement might be like 'even above nature'. And exceptional deeds, extreme endurance, courage and commitment are the sublime in human action.

Amongst the immediate artistic consequences of the spread of this concept was an infatuation with wild places and the development of the means to depict them, and a preoccupation with epic (real or imaginary). And concomitantly, a fascination with super-human courage, cruelty and power. The rhetoric of political violence, of terrible beauty, from St Just to Pádraig Pearse and beyond, is constructed upon models of sublimity. In architectural terms, geometrical simplicity, 'uniformity', 'vastness' and 'repetition' are the preconditions of sublime power. At a later stage, industrial technology came to be seen as awesome and astonishing, as the work of superhuman or mythical agencies.

As we shall find, the sublime plays an important part in the representation of heritage, both the sublimity of wild nature, and the sublimity of mythical history – and the intersections between them. Examples will be studied later in this book, when the ideological function of sublimity will be analysed. It will be useful, therefore, to look at the seminal moment in the history of the concept.

James Macpherson's 'Ossian' poems (1760–62) are normally studied as curiosities. They present, in high-flown rhythmic prose, a grandiose vision of a Celtic past which is inextricably mingled with typically eighteenth-century preoccupations. Their fraudulent aspect, their instantaneous and highly influential popularity, and their repercussions (even down to this day), have always deflected interest from their ideological function. This was primarily to propose an alternative history for Western Europe by constructing an alternative prehistory. Celticism was to be seen as a rival to classicism. The cultural (and indeed political) challenge of such a proposal was immense and had immense appeal (and this appeal has by no means vanished today). It is one of the means by which a 'periphery' revenges itself upon a defining 'centre'.[38]

Macpherson's aim was, in its better part, to re-assert the historical and social values of his own Gaelic-speaking origins; as a child he had witnessed the 1745 uprising in the Highlands and its consequences. Amongst these was the progressive decay of the

38. Chapman's argument, in its briefest form, is that the 'Celts' 'have not found themselves by chance on the edges of someone else's world, but have been historiographically constituted as peripheral, and this condition is a fundamental feature of their definition'. op. cit., p. 95.

language, from both compulsion and choice; so for Macpherson to collect and write down oral traditions and to study old manuscripts (which he undoubtedly did) was an activity with some political content.[39] At the same time he was ambitious for a literary career in English, and aware that the changes in the Highlands could never be reversed. He wrote that:

> Many have now learned to leave their mountains, and seek their fortunes in a milder climate; and though a certain *amor patriae* may sometimes bring them back, they have, during their absence, imbibed enough of foreign manners to despise the customs of their ancestors. (Preface to *Fingal*)[40]

Thus the foundations of the 'Ossian' poems contained incompatible intentions which could only be resolved by lifting the original oral traditions out of the context in which Macpherson encountered them and inserting them into a conjectural history, which owed little to contemporary scholarship.

> It was, of course, advantageous to Macpherson as a creative writer; the Celts were a vanished people, whose greatness was magnified by the mystery surrounding them. At the same time, Macpherson's imagination was unhampered by inconvenient facts: his conjectural history was really a personal view of the Ancient World which he wished others to share.[41]

Following this strategy were a train of assumptions about the origins of language, ancient migrations and parallels with the *Iliad* and other classical sources which are not germane to this study; though it is interesting that ancient Germany was seen in a similar light to ancient Scotland and Ireland. What we find ourselves reading, in the introductions to the poems, is a prescription for European primitivism, with as yet undiscovered entailments.

This primitivism is a core element in the growth of nineteenth-century nationalism and the invention of traditions. 'Ossian' in effect provides a template for the creation of other national epics, more or less validly based upon really existing material, but departing from that material in greater or lesser degrees. The Finnish 'Kalevala' cycle (first published in 1835 and used as part of the drive toward 'national style' in the 1890s) is another example. Similar epics appeared in Old Slavonic and Breton.

In an Irish context we think of the uses made of the *Táin* and the figure of Cúchulainn. Though the story of the *Táin* was not widely known before the publication of O'Grady's *History of Ireland* (vol. 2, *Cúchulain and his Contemporaries* 1880), it was rapidly taken up by nationalists.

39. Some of the historiographical problems of the Celtic languages and their 'decay' are discussed by Chapman (1992); see his ch. 6 and ch. 8. Much of the writing around this problem he condemns for 'gullible self-righteousness' in which 'serious and unbiased study of the way the socio-linguistic world *truly* works for a bilingual is typically lacking' (p. 102).

40. In the account of Macpherson I am indebted to F.J. Stafford *The Sublime Savage: a Study of James Macpherson and the Poems of Ossian* (Edinburgh UP 1988), see p. 58 and ch. 9.

41. Ibid., p. 152.

What was remarkable about the Cúchulainn saga for them was less its antiquarian nature than its modern relevance. The saga could be seen as a challenge to Irish political subservience to England and to modern 'materialistic' values.[42]

42. Turpin, J. 'Cúchulainn Lives On', *CIRCA*, 69 Autumn 1994, p. 27.

That the hero was, in point of myth, defending Ulster against the 'men of Ireland' was an irony lost upon Pádraig Pearse, who made an imaginative conflation of the epic warrior with the figure of Christ (which carries over into Oliver Sheppard's sculpture). The ancient defence of Ulster has not been forgotten, however, by 'loyalist' paramilitaries in Northern Ireland who have adapted the hero to their quite different purposes.

Perhaps the most significant artistic use of ancient source material is the libretto and score of Richard Wagner's *Ring des Nibelungen* (libretto 1847–51, score completed by 1876), in which the most primitive 'Teutonic' material available is delivered and developed in an advanced, even 'modernist', musical idiom.

In the more intense versions of cultural nationalism, the nation itself is placed in a sublime category, as a fact of nature, beyond history and therefore beyond question. What follows from this is that historical change when it occurs can only be the result of external agencies, and can only be bad. Thus Synge writes of the Aran Islands:

> The thought that this island will gradually yield to the ruthlessness of 'progress' is as the certainty that decaying age is moving always nearer the cheeks it is your ecstacy to kiss. How much of Ireland was formerly like this and how much of Ireland is today Anglicised and civilised and brutalised.[43]

43. *Collected Works*, Price A. (ed.) (Oxford UP 1965), vol. 2 p. 103, quoted by Watson, op. cit.

Thus the inhabitants can only play a passive role, and 'Celticism', like any other ethnicism, lifts one's consciousness out of the problems of real history. (Lest any English readers should have a lingering complacency in these matters, let them consider the anxieties expressed, all through this century, about the increasing 'Americanisation' of the English 'way of life', and the 'decay of old values'.)[44]

44. See numerous passages in Wiener, M. *English Culture and the Decline of the Industrial Spirit 1850–1980* (Cambridge U.P. 1981).

And at the same time, we need to see the inspiration of Macpherson as extending to more scholarly, less ambiguous, activities; for there is no doubt that the enthusiasm for 'Ossian' proved a great spur to antiquarian and early-historical studies, and to the study of folklore, languages and the ancient foundations of European culture. Of particular importance here would be such publications as the *Deutsche Mythologie* by the Grimm brothers in 1835; and in an Irish context, the founding of the Gaelic Society of Dublin in 1807, the first of several study groups, and important essays on early architecture and design, such as George Petrie's book *On the Ecclesiastical Architecture of Ireland* (1845). Petrie has been described as

> [T]he founder of systematic and scientific archaeology in Ireland . . . [countering] two tendencies among historians of Ireland. On the one hand there were those who claimed that the native Irish were savages, and had always been so . . . On the other hand there were those who developed glamorous accounts of ancient Ireland from the more colourful flights of the Irish bards.[45]

45. Sheehy, op. cit., p. 20.

Another important scholarly enterprise that seems to have had some Ossianic inspiration was the Harpist's Festival organised by the McCracken family and friends in Belfast in the summer of 1792. The aim of this was to

> [R]evive and perpetuate the Ancient Music and Poetry of Ireland . . . to assemble the Harpers, those descendants of our Ancient Bards, who are at present almost exclusively possessed of all that remains of the Music, Poetry and oral traditions of Ireland . . .[46]

46. Prospectus, as quoted in McNeil, M. *The Life and Times of Mary Ann McCracken 1770–1886* (Belfast, Blackstaff 1988), p. 78.

This event led to the publication of Edward Bunting's first collection of Irish airs (in 1797). That it should have been organised by a circle of friends actively engaged both in revolutionary politics and the most advanced industrial development in Ireland is typical. Their use of the phrase 'oral traditions' (now a standard phrase of the heritage industry) is the earliest known to this author.

These scholarly attempts to come to grips with early national origins were accompanied by attempts at suitable visual representations. Joseph Peacock (1783–1837) and Daniel Maclise (1806–1870) both made paintings on the grand scale, paintings that unite sublime emotions with archaeological detail. Petrie's own paintings are also typical of the period, combining painstaking historical accuracy with picturesque conventions.

We can now begin to see something of the ideological function of the sublime. Viewed, as it were, from 'within', it was a compensatory device whereby the displaced and damaged could restore a sense of self-worth. 'They [the 'Celts'] provided the constricted, pathetically small nation, which had little to recommend it in its present state, with an unimaginably grandiose past, by way of consolation.[47] And at the same time, frequently within the same minds, it was a spur to real scholarship and historical enquiry, creating a genuinely historical foundation for national feelings that had real consequences.

47. Morgan, P., op. cit., p. 69.

Viewed from 'without', the sublime worked to de-historicise and render fanciful, real and sometimes urgent, political challenges. The political challenge being, in the case of Macpherson, and subsequently, what to do with the Celtic 'fringe'. In 1757, when

Burke's essay was published, the Highlands constituted a perceived threat (more perceived than actual) to the established triad of Edinburgh, Dublin and London. In 1762, the 'Ossian' poems were an intervention into the politics of Scots influence over Westminster and were clearly understood as such. By rendering Scotland (and by extension, Ireland) as sublime, Macpherson was putting them beyond the pale of rational discourse. The Celtic 'fringe' was being created as the 'Other' to the norm of the Anglo-Scottish settlement and Enlightenment ideology.

Thus the sublime – as it appears in Burke's *Essay* and then just a little later in the 'Ossian' poems – acts as a defining stage in the 'writing' of the Highlands and islands. The Celtic 'fringe' is both defined by this writing and thereby separated from the cultural and political 'mainland' of the newly united kingdom. This is a continuance of a 'writing' established in the previous century, whose ideological function was to give moral validation to the suppression of native Irish and wild clansmen.[48] In this context, the sublime is a part of the much larger geo-political and economic stance which required an absolute control over the 'western approaches', by any means whatsoever.[49]

We are, of course, dealing here with the effects of the texts in question; we cannot be certain of either Burke's or Macpherson's 'intentions' which were presumably mixed and only partly conscious, and in any case have little bearing on the subsequent reading of their books. The important matter is the reception and wide distribution of both the *Essay* and 'Ossian'.

This interpretation of the sublime may seem at first at some distance from an analysis of 'heritage'; but as we shall see, that is far from the case. The sublime promoted and fed the growing field of antiquarianism, and demanded attempts to give it visual form. Representations of history, especially ancient history, are almost inseparable from sublimity. And in so far as the sublime fed nationalist (in this case 'Celticist') cultural aspirations, so far could it be used to construct an ahistorical national 'heritage'.

The evocation of the ancient past as a national heritage will be studied in greater depth through buildings which are notably 'sublime' in concept and execution. At that point we will have to consider, with some subtlety, the positive uses of sublimity, and ask to what degree the sense of awe and astonishment may be a liberating experience rather than a means of covert subordination and disablement. We shall also have to analyse the unconsidered assumption of sublimity, and to ask to what degree its values, like those of the picturesque, have been internalised as unconscious premises by the creators and constructors of heritage.

48. See Cairns and Richards, (eds.) op. cit., esp. ch. 1.

49. See also Brett, D. catalogue essay in *Ireland: Poetic Land, Political Territory* (Northern Centre for Contemporary Art, Sunderland 1995). Cairns and Richards fail to comment on this obvious correlation. Ireland was for centuries the back door through which to threaten the British state, and the control of deep-water harbours facing the North Atlantic has been essential for survival in two world wars. To this very day, Dalriada remains stuffed with NATO submarine bases, long runways and defence establishments.

Two further aspects of the sublime are important – the sublimity of real landscape and 'national landscapes', and that of technology.

Macpherson's publications did more than anything else to fix the idea of natural sublimity in European formal culture. Wild landscapes acquired an immense status in painting, literature, and garden design as correlatives of extreme states of mind and life. It becomes possible to speak of an 'iconology' of wilderness.[50] Certain landscapes, and representions of landscapes, acquired iconic status as the bearers of special (usually national historical) meanings, and a chain of connections can often be traced from certain key images down through their reproduction in print form, to photography, to postcards and tourist brochures. All over Europe, using both picturesque and sublime exemplars, certain landscapes came to be designated as 'national'. Their supposed 'authenticity' symbolised the authenticity of people and nation as natural categories.

50. See Cosgrove, D. and Daniels, S. (eds.) *The Iconography of Landscape: Essays on the Symbolic Representation, Design and Use of Past Environments* (Cambridge UP 1988), intro.

Once again, the west of Ireland affords typical examples, down to the present day, in which national character and sublimity are conflated. Writings and brochures are published in which photography portrays a land of mountains and lakes as devoid of human activity as a painting by Paul Henry. That this 'emptiness' is a consequence of emigration and famine cannot, of course, enter into the discourse, because that would be to intrude substantial history into the process of aestheticisation. Yet this 'emptiness' is one of the principal rhetorical features of Henry's landscapes, which progressively lose their human inhabitants and become, finally, evocations of water, rock and weather.

(As a digression, it is interesting to compare the uses of sublimity in Ireland with the picturesque concept of a rural and harmonious England – 'small, as our landscape is small, it is sweet picturesque homely farmyardish', etc. – and the elevation of these sentiments into a national dogma. [*See* chapter 3.] In this context we can interpret the paintings of Constable and their now iconic status in some English minds as part of the anti-industrial spirit analysed by Martin Wiener.[51])

51. Wiener, op. cit., esp. ch. 4.

This nationalist aestheticising has been very widespread. Something similar may be seen in the uses of landscape painting for the construction of a Canadian national identity. To put the matter very briefly, early paintings of Canada by European artists were made according to the picturesque and sublime conventions of the time, with native Canadians playing the part of the peasants and heroic 'extras'. But by the beginning of this century a demand had arisen for an appropriate 'Canadian' school. By 1920 the 'Group of Seven' held an exhibition whose catalogue proclaimed that:

The group of seven artists whose pictures are here exhibited have for several years held a like vision concerning Art in Canada. They are all imbued with the idea that an Art must grow and flower in the land before the country will be a real home for its people.[52]

The painters in question became known for a particular view of Canada as a vast, unpeopled and sublime 'Northland', partly modelled upon Scandinavian paintings of similar scenes – a late flowering of romantic sublimity which was, typically enough, endowed with a mixture of racial propaganda and mysticism. Such an imagery could not, of course, encompass the very great real variety of the country; their project failed, but not before creating a substantial body of work that still resonates, and which continues to feed tourist imagery. The wider challenge, of creating a meaningful 'Canadian' imagery, remains in conflict with both international and separatist/regional ambitions.

What I describe as 'the technological sublime' is of less relevance to our main concern, but the representation of technology and science, especially in their military aspects and in the domain of real or imagined outer space, is now a *locus classicus* of contemporary sublimity. It has, moreover, some bearing upon the presentation of 'industrial heritage'.

The vast size, repetition, uniformity and apparently superhuman powers of industry have, from the very first, been seen in mythical terms. The Wye valley, primal scene of the English picturesque, was also a scene of forges and mechanical hammers, and the romantic gorge was made more romantic by echoing to beaten metal. 'Machinery,' wrote Thomas Whately, 'especially when its powers are stupendous, or its effect formidable, is an effort of art, which may be accommodated to the extravagancies of nature.' And Gilpin, at the same spot, observed that

> All the employments of the people seem to require either exertion or caution; and the idea of force or of danger which attend them, gives to the scene an animation . . . perfectly compatible with the wildest romantic situations.[53]

Arthur Young, visiting Coalbrookdale in 1785, contrasted the beauty of the wooded hills with

> [T]hat variety of horrors art has spread at the bottom; the noise of forges, mills etc., with all their vast machinery, the flames bursting from the furnaces with the burning of the coal and the smoak of the limekilns, are altogether sublime, and would unite well with craggy and bare rocks . . .

From these perceptions grew a new painterly subject matter – the depiction of industry in picturesque or sublime terms – and a new

52. Osborne, B.S. 'The Iconography of Nationhood in Canadian Art', in Cosgrove and Daniels, (eds.), op. cit., p. 169.

53. Andrews, op. cit., p. 93.

range of graphic conventions. Paul Sandby and and John Cotman both applied watercolour techniques to industrial subjects, and a host of illustrators and draughtsmen adapted picturesque manners to technological subjects. The most sublime and self-consciously grand painter of the early nineteenth century, John Martin, adapted industrial imagery to apocalyptic themes.[54]

To compare the operations of industry to the labours of Titans or the Cyclops (and so to embed them in the formal culture they were about to destroy) becomes a stock response. This mythical imagery remains, to this day, predominant in many areas of colossal technology; especially in military and space hardware.

The imagery transmitted back from space vehicles, and the imagery of serious and not-so-serious science fiction films, feed a continuing appetite for the sublime. The qualities of immensity, extremity, geometrical precision and superhuman power are caught in the naming of rocketry (*Atlas, Saturn, Challenger, Energeia, Kosmos*). The visual conventions and rituals that surround the representation of the space industries (both in reality and in fiction) are the descendants of the early industrial paintings; the world of steam and speed in which the products of human ingenuity and capital are endowed with the numinous power of uncontrolled nature. The naming and representation of military hardware follows the same pattern; the wilder parts of Britain now echo to the rumble of the Fairchild Republic A-10A *Thunderbolt* and the howl of the Panavia MRCA *Tornado*.[55]

My aim in these chapters has been to establish the foundations of the 'heritage' concept, and trace the origins of some of the typical assumptions and attitudes we encounter today. I believe I have shown in sufficient detail that aspects of heritage have a long prehistory, both in the development of taste and in the development of specific practices. In chapter 4 I propose to bring together these several different kinds of representations and ally them with a short study of public spectacle. I propose that the amalgamation of antiquarian interests and aesthetic categories in the form of popular entertainment, which took place in expositions and spectacular events throughout the later part of the nineteenth century, forms the foundation of all subsequent heritage display, and that the move from an *image-scarce* culture to one that is *image-saturated* is the major stage on the road to the 'society of the spectacle'.

54. For an extensive survey, see Klingender, F. *Art and the Industrial Revolution* (London, Evelyn, Adams Mackay Ltd 1968).

55. See Patrick Eyres's 'Classic Ground; a confrontation with the military sublime', *CIRCA*, 43 Dec. 1989, pp. 18–22.

4

THE TECHNOLOGIES OF REPRESENTATION

In chapters 2 and 3 I described something of the 'prehistory' of our topic; the existence of artistic and architectural antiquarianism and of aesthetic concepts which, I argued, are part of the construction of contemporary ideas of 'heritage'. My intention now is to describe some of the developments in communications media and image reproduction, in entertainment, and in display, which, in association with the above, actually made possible present-day displays of heritage. This chapter will lay stress, once again, upon the early years of the nineteenth century, and describe how these elements came together to create and publicise events such as the Great Exhibitions of the later part of the century; it was on such occasions, and by such combinatorial means, that the first heritage displays were created. This chapter traces the increasingly visual character of industrial culture toward its present 'spectacular' condition.

In some degree I am dealing with what Daniel Boorstein has described as the 'graphic revolution' which, through its indefinite expansion of reproductions, destroys the sense of original reality and replaces it by 'pseudo-events' and 'image-thinking'.[1] His entertaining polemic, however, generates no critical position because it offers no explanatory structure; it is an example of the forlorn conservatism that limps along behind consumer capitalism, nagging, and altering nothing.[2]

The chapter is in two sections. In the first I deal with the technology of image reproduction and distribution; and in the second with the technology of the spectacle and development of spectacular events such as exhibitions. The two are linked under the general headings of *visualisation* and *simulation*.

In a chapter of this scope these matters can be dealt with in only a summary manner, but I do not believe this falsifies the general picture. Furthermore, though I shall lay initial stress upon the technology of representation, the technology is not a neutral medium through which, transparently, a message passes unaltered from sender to receiver. It is itself a participant in the creation of the meaning.

1. See Boorstein, D. *The Image; a Guide to Pseudo-Events in America* (New York, Vintage Books 1992 edn., first edn. 1961).

2. For a more complete discussion of Boorstin's argument, see McCandless (1976) ch. 5.

This is true in both a shallow and a deep sense. The same event, described through the spoken word, the written word, the drawing, the photograph, the panorama, the tableau, the theatrical performance and the film, is delivered, experienced and understood through different senses and capacities, and according to different conventions. But though the comparative understanding of a drawing and a photograph requires different kinds and degrees of visual acuity, these differences are not *merely* matters of convention that can be learnt, taken up, abandoned and forgotten at will. They each imply, and are embedded in, systems of construing the world. Each technology of communication and the medium it employs is, in this respect, what Ernst Cassirer describes as a 'symbolic form', in which values and assumptions are inscribed prior to any putative message. These values and assumptions are the formative power in any medium, over and above any putative informative function they may be called on to perform.[3] I regard this symbolic form as prior to the particular visual ideology presented through the particular medium, it being the grounding or necessary condition of the existence of the ideology.

The camera, for example, is conceived upon and propagates a theory of vision and an epistemology which, in the 1840s, seemed to make naturalistic drawing redundant; but it only did so to those who thought that drawing the world depended upon and propagated the same system of ideas. It was invented on the analogy of well-established perceptual theories that ultimately rest upon John Locke's account of sense-data 'writing' upon our minds as if upon a blank sheet of paper. It was then interpreted according to current positivist concepts of 'fact' and immediately acquired the authority of 'truth' and 'accuracy', because it demonstrated the truth criteria according to which it had been conceived. If one had internalised these criteria as assumptions, the camera *had* to be regarded as superior in truth and accuracy to the unaided eye and hand. This was, of course, a broadly ideological position, part of a wider concept of utilitarian modernity; and thus precipitated an artistic crisis, the effects of which still echo around us. But the camera has come subsequently to be understood as a much more subtle instrument, capable of many and varied meanings.

Different image reproduction systems, likewise, carry with them formative powers that are greater than mere technique; each creates different forms of understanding in the recipient mind. And the gathering together of individuals as witnesses to the spectacles of representation – either actual spectacles, as in large exhibitions, or virtual spectacles, as in dioramas, panoramas and ultimately in film and television (not to mention more recent technologies) – are formative of new social relations. And these new social relations are

3. See Cassirer, E. *Language and Myth* (New York, Dover Press 1946); and also McLuhan, M. *Understanding Media* (London, Routledge Kegan Paul 1964) for more general discussion of these questions.

themselves formative of new understandings, not least of nation-ality and history.

The first decades of the nineteenth century witnessed an 'image explosion' of an unprecedented kind. In 1800 imagery was either unique (as in paintings) or confined to small editions, and the printer's workshop was much as it had been two hundred years before; by the time of the Great Exhibition of 1851, imagery was ubiquitous and cheap and sustained by a highly organised graphic industry. A 'graphic revolution' had, indeed, occurred; and it has augmented ever since.

This 'explosion' has been studied in its parts, but never as a single object of study.[4] Yet it is an event inseparable from and necessary to the process of industrialisation and the creation of a modern state; and it appears to presage and accompany a modification in human understanding as great as that which took place with the Gutenberg revolution. The event (and it was so swift that it may decently be described as an event) was the change from an *image-scarce* culture to one that is *image-saturated*.

4. With the exception of Boorstin, whose inadequacies I have already indicated, Marshal McLuhan's writings provide an essential starting point for much of what follows, but his intentions are different from mine.

I: Speaking to the Eye

In October of 1851 the *Spectator* published an unsigned article entitled 'Speaking to the Eye'; it presents us with a conceptual landscape that has to be explored:

> Those whose office it is to dispense instruction are practising a new art. Our great authors are now artists. They speak to the eye and the language is fascinating and impressive . . . and so popular is this mode of communication, that illustrated newspapers are becoming common all over Europe. . . . The causes and consequences of this dawning and important change are worthy of notice.[5]

5. *The Spectator*, 9, 1851, p. 533 *et seq.*

After a survey of the progress of the *Illustrated London News*, the writer summarises the developments in wood engraving and other techniques, such that 'illustrative engravings can be given to the public at one-fortieth of their cost a few years ago'. But it is not the causes that we should study, but the probable consequences, because

> pictorial representation may at once convey totally different and totally new ideas to the mind. The artist speaks a universal language. A Turk or Chinese understands him at once . . . hence it has become practical to establish in London, French and German journals, which, by means

of illustrations, speak at once to the natives of France and Germany. Pictures, then, have the great advantage over words, that they convey immediately much new knowledge to the mind; they are equivalent, in proportion as they approach perfection, to seeing the objects themselves; and they are universally comprehended. They make everyone participate in the gathered knowledge of all . . . If the modern improvements in the art of transmitting knowledge . . . be more efficacious in diffusing knowledge than the art of printing words, may we not expect it to be the forerunner of changes greater than printing has hitherto brought forward.

Exhibitions and displays have a similar power: 'The Great Exhibition itself, which is a representation to the eye . . . is performing the office of a large illustrated newspaper . . . it speaks all tongues.' But it would be a feeble instrument without the assistance of illustration and letter-press, 'without which it is doubtful if it could itself ever have existed'.

A complete exegesis of this text, down to the details of style, would be an illuminating and extensive task that has to be foregone. We are concerned here with the relation that develops between the printed image, spectacle, tourism and national aggrandisement – by means of 'representations to the eye'. Where printed imagery alone is concerned a simple strategy of three main themes is proposed – the *means*, the *pictorial conventions*, and the *occasions*.[6]

6. All that follows is a digest of ch. 2 of Brett (1984) where more complete research can be found; it is indebted to studies by Fox (1974), Houfe (1978), Ivins (1953), Jussim (1974), Lindley (1970), Lilien (1972), Marzio (1980), Portenaar (1933), Rosner (1951), Steinberg (1959) and Wakeman (1973).

7. Moles, A. *Information Theory and Aesthetic Perception* (Carbondale, Univ. of Illinois Press 1968), p. 197.

The knowing reader may recognise in this something akin to the *channel*, *code*, and *message* of information theory. But information theory declines to discuss the wider problems of meaning. 'Meaning', writes Moles, 'rests on a set of conventions which are a priori to the receptor and the transmitter. Thus it is not transmitted . . .'[7] But it is precisely the overall meaning, the 'symbolic form' of this image explosion that engages our attention.

One conclusion will be that the overall meaning, and function, of this image explosion was the restructuring of pre-industrial attitudes and forms of knowledge into shapes and relations suitable to the new industrial society, something comparable to the time-discipline described by Andrew Ure. That is to say, its significance was epistemological and its function ideological; it was a major element in the 'catastrophic' transformation towards modernity.

Means

If we begin with 'means' this is not to imply that in some mysteriously simple sense a technical invention 'causes' cultural development. What the *Economist* describes as 'great changes in society' belong to a different order of explanation and nexus of causality than do 'discoveries and inventions that are almost unnoticed at their origins'.

The mechanisation of printing through the use of revolving cylinders, at first to bear the paper and then, after some delay, to bear the type-forme, seems to have arisen because of the insatiable demand for more text more quickly. *The Times* was constantly occupied with this problem and commissioned and spent large sums of money upon several schemes to speed the process. The Koenig and Bowers machine of 1814, the automatic feed, and the cylindrical type-forme, arose directly from the belief that there was a very large potential readership. In this sense the specific technology was a response and not a cause. But the principal mechanical inventions that made cylinder printing possible took place in the textile printing industry several years before. Thomas Bell's patent for a textile printer of 1784 has all the parts – in a rudimentary form – that are be found on present day industrial gravure presses. Bell was by trade a pictorial engraver on copper, an occupation that lay in between several areas of importance to this study. Moreover, other factors of a quite different kind could hasten or delay the chain of invention. The tax on printed text (per sheet of paper) delayed the continuous printing of text on rolled and cut paper, and Koenig's first machines were rejected in Germany because 'they will issue many impressions, but nothing beautiful'.

However, we can isolate important moments and inventions that created the conditions, without which an explosion of imagery would have been impossible, without attempting to draw simple causal conclusions either way.

The first of these is the mechanisation of paper production, first in single sheets and then in rolls (1837). Rosner (1951) gives some figures for the resulting reductions in cost. A second is the improvement of press design. In 1813 the new Stanhope machine used by the *Leeds Mercury* could print at a rate of 250 imp. p.h.; but by 1820, the Koenig and Bowers press could work at 1,000 imp. p.h. and was driven by a small steam engine. For higher quality printing (particularly for printed books) the Hopkinson and Cope platen presses were available from 1830. At the Great Exhibition of 1851 an Applegarth and Cowper machine could be seen throwing off the *Illustrated London News* at 5,000 imp. p.h. 'Illustrative engravings can now be given to the public at one-fortieth of their cost a few years ago.'

A more complete attention, however, must be paid to the nature of the printed image, to the combination of image and text, and the type-compatibility that wood-block engraving made easy. Although it could be fitted into the forme along with the type, the box-wood block might seem an unlikely medium for an image explosion. Engraving on wood is a demanding craft, apparently unsuited to swift production. To get engraved blocks completed on time for the new journals, teams of engravers were employed in an elaborate division of labour. A considerable industry grew up around the creation of these blocks, whose organisation is still not fully understood. But what gave wood-engraving such predominance was the durability of the original block, and before long the technique of casting or electrotyping copies of it in lead ('stereotyping' as it was called). This prolonged the life of the original engraving by many times – millions of impressions could come from a single cut. By these means, journals such as the *Penny Magazine* were being reprinted in New York, during 1836, from stereotypes of the original London editions.

In the more expensive areas of printing, engraving on metal was advanced quantitatively by the change from copper to steel plates; the much greater hardness of steel permitted it to be put through the press more often and at greater speed, enabling some thousands of 'pulls' to be taken, whereas copper was restricted to hundreds or less. The publisher and artistic entrepreneur Rudolf Ackermann was prominent in this area of work, extending his business from hand-tinted picturesque aquatints to mass-produced albums and annuals illustrated with steel engravings. Titles such as his *Forget-Me-Not* ran from 1822 to 1847 in editions of several thousand. Alaric Watts commissioned original paintings and drawings to illustrate his *Literary Souvenir* which ran from 1826 to 1842 with a 6,000 imprint. Altogether over 300 separate annuals and similar works appeared between 1823 and 1855. John Martin and J.M.W. Turner were among the very many artists whose imagery was distributed through this medium to a much wider, though still not 'popular', market, establishing a canon of sentimental and picturesque taste amongst the middle classes which has hardly altered to this day. This included historical tales and easy versions of national history. An interesting enquiry can be made into the dependence of painters on engraving, and the effect of this upon the development or lack of development of style. Walter Benjamin was to comment, 'To an even greater extent, the work of art reproduced becomes the work of art designed for reproduction.'[8]

The reproduction of imagery became a major industrial activity in the 1830s, and high wages were paid and high fees changed hands:

> Sums of money that sound preposterous were lavished upon the several departments . . . amounts varying from 20 to 150 guineas were paid to artists for the loan of pictures to be engraved, and it was by no means uncommon for the engraver to receive 150 guineas for the production of a single plate.[9]

8. Benjamin, W. 'The Work of Art in the Age of Mechanical Reproduction' in *Illuminations* (London Fontana, 1970), p. 226.

9. S.C. Hall, publisher of *The Amulet*, quoted by Houfe (1978) p. 41.

The upmarket reproductive engravers, accustomed to working on a large format for separately issued editions, found their livelihoods under threat from what were described as 'ignorant capitalists' producing picture-books and collections of old masters. In 1836 the House of Commons Select Committee on Arts was petitioned by engravers seeking full membership of the Royal Academy in order to protect their status. Witnesses averred that there were now five times as many engravers as there had been twenty years before, and that their importance in disseminating art had been overlooked. In cities such as Leeds the four printers and one engraver who were recorded in trade directories from 1800 were increased to forty-two and twenty-eight respectively by 1854, having at their disposal printing presses of vastly greater speed and productivity.[10]

From the uncertain figures available, we can estimate that for every image printed from a metal plate in 1800, there were 100 in 1836 (*increase x 100*); and for every engraving on woodblock in 1817 a threefold increase in the number of engravers and a very great increase in the number (n) of impressions from each block or stereotype suggests an *increase of 3n*. The effect of this upon the production and trading of unique imagery (painting of all kinds) and of small limited edition imagery (etching etc.) may be surmised. We are accustomed to regarding the invention of photography as having modified seriously the nature and role of unique imagery, but with these figures in mind we should reconsider that view. The industrialisation of image reproduction significantly pre-dates the invention of photography.

Lithography was less easily mechanised and remained slower than woodblock engraving until the 1850s; its principal functions were the introduction of effective colour reproduction and the freeing of letter-forms from their dependence upon cast type. By lithographic means, image and text could be given an iconic unity that was very quickly exploited by commercial advertising. Furthermore, the adaptability of lithography, its relative absence of distinct character, could be turned to commercial advantage. Marzio (1979) gives the following advertisement from 1849:

> Duval's Lithographic and Colour Printing Establishment of Philadelphia. Drawings of all kinds executed on stone. Copper and steel plates, woodcuts, manuscripts etc. transferred. All kinds of colour or ornamented printing executed in the neatest style. Nota: engineers and surveyors, wishing to execute their drawings for transferring will be supplied with suitable paper and ink. Having succeeded in adapting for the first time Steam Power to the lithographic press, extensive orders and the largest size drawings can be printed with great despatch and moderate cost.[11]

10. See Brett (1984). The first paper mill in Leeds was recorded in 1823; there were eight by 1851; printers' suppliers are also recorded.

11. Marzio, P. *The Democratic Art: Chromolithography 1840–1900* (London, Scholar Press 1979), fig. 3. p. 25. Marzio comments that the claims for mechanisation were probably an exaggeration at that time (1849). Mechanised lithography did not take off until Sigl's patent in 1852.

So far I have discussed only the printing of autographic images – those produced by the hand of some graphic artist (albeit often mediated by several other hands as well). Photography must now be considered.

At the time of the Great Exhibition the photographic 'explosion' had barely begun. Gernsheim gives a figure of fifty-one registered photographers in London in that year, followed by 2,879 ten years later.[12] To take Leeds again as a typical British example, the number rose from three in 1850 to twenty-two in 1857. But here the figures conceal much information, since it comes from commercial sources only. In the case of Leeds (and we may assume like cases elsewhere) commercial photography in the form of the making of daguerreotypes was at first the monopoly of one man, Samuel Topham. He (like so many other figures in this story) was an engraver who had established a 'Photographic Portrait Gallery' on the strength of a ten-year licence to use Daguerre's process within the city boundaries. When the patent lapsed in 1852, other people rushed into business with new processes. Pharmacists found it profitable to become photographic suppliers and in 1853 one of these pharmacists had diversified, and was offering for sale a 'tourist camera' for amateur use (possibly the first of its kind).

A similar story can be told of Belfast, which illustrates the alacrity with which news of Daguerre's invention spread. The *Newsletter* of 19 February, 1839 carried a long article on the Frenchman's achievement (i.e. within six weeks of Daguerre's recognition by the French state). By September of the same year, a local engraver, F.S. Beatty, wrote on the same topic describing his own experiments, and a year later exhibited a 'photogenic drawing' of one of the city's bridges. In August 1842 Beatty and a partner sold off the engraving business and established themselves as portrait photographers at an address in Castle Street in the centre of the town. Subsequently, a profession of photographer came into being, with nineteen recorded firms in 1861, eighty-three in 1881, and 234 by 1901. Beatty is known to have experimented with photo-lithography later in the century.[13]

The cost of photographs decreased (in Leeds, again) from 10s.6d. in 1842 to 2s. in 1855 according to the invoices of the Photographic Portrait Gallery. The speed of the process had increased notably, but the essential invention was the glass negative, the master image of a very large number of potential replica prints.

Though photography was some way from being incorporated into an industry by 1851, all the components and processes of industrial production and distribution were coming together. A study of the previous employments of the commercial photographers of Leeds and

12. Gernsheim, H. and A. *The History of Photography* . . . (1955) p. 166. I am also indebted to a pamphlet of the Leeds City Art Gallery, *Early Photography in Leeds*, (1981). The figures for Belfast come from Walker, B.M. *Shadows on Glass* (Belfast, Appletree Press 1976).

13. McCaughan, M. 'Francis Beatty, Ireland's first Commercial Photographer', in *Source* vol. 2, 2, 1995, p. 6.

district gives a picture of the intermarrying of skills at the start of this new aspect of the image industry. By tracing back names in the trade directories we discover that they had been, and often still were, engravers, pharmacists, opticians, watchmakers, cabinet-makers, booksellers (who were often printers and publishers), art dealers and artists. This is a perfect cross-section of the skills that a photographic and later a film industry would require. Leeds, was, in fact, one of the first cities to be recorded on moving film.

It was also a profile of the skills required for the forthcoming marriage between photographic and mechanical print processes. Fortunately it is not necessary to discuss here the bewildering elaboration of new inventions which brought about the growth of our present panoply of image systems; instead we can now propose a simple staged diagram.

After a first stage of primitive unique image making (1), manual printing is devised from the textile and metal-working crafts (2). This manual stage is succeeded by a mechanical stage in the early nineteenth century through the adaptation of machines originally conceived for textile printing; but the original master image is still 'autographic'(3). Simultaneously a photographic system is invented (4) and developed by negative/positive printing (5). After much trial and error, photographic images are rendered capable of mechanical reproduction – giving a 'photo-mechanical' stage (6). Distribution by telegraphy and radio add a further stage (7), rapidly overtaken by the electronic media, which are not strictly speaking print media at all, but image storage and distribution channels (8).

At each stage there is a great increase in the quantity of imagery in circulation, but the new means do not drive out the old (or, only briefly), because each technology is also a 'symbolic form' embodying not merely visual conventions, but to repeat, *a way of construing the world*. Primitive autography (painting and drawing), manual printing (etching and engraving) are still with us. The early stages of photography are once again being 'rediscovered'. Wood engraving is frequently 'revived'. The black and white film is now something special. At each stage the earlier 'superseded' media have undergone a change in function toward a greater specialisation, or artistic usage.

Such are some of the technical *means* by which the 'society of the spectacle' has been brought into being.

4.1 Diagram to illustrate the successive stages of image production and replication and the persistence of older means within the overall system.

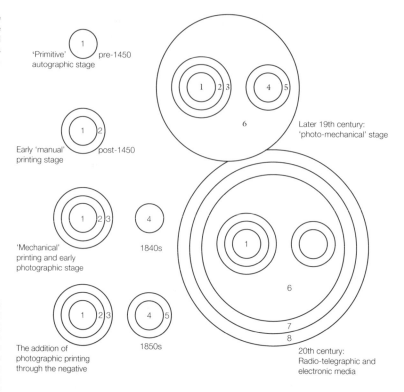

'Primitive' autographic stage   pre-1450

Early 'manual' printing stage   post-1450

'Mechanical' printing and early photographic stage   1840s

The addition of photographic printing through the negative   1850s

Later 19th century: 'photo-mechanical' stage

20th century: Radio-telegraphic and electronic media

4.2 The 'code' of the wood engraving: detail of an illustration of the living conditions of Famine victims in 1847, taken from the Illustrated London News (see chapter 5). The characteristic cuts of the engraver's knife follow a tracing made by another craftsman from drawings made by the original artist-reporter. Compare with the dot code of the halftone plate or the television screen.

4.3 Enlarged detail of newspaper photograph, showing dot structure.

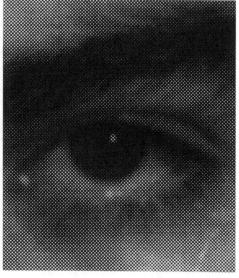

Pictorial Conventions

By pictorial conventions is meant (at the *macro* level) those ground rules and cues for the comprehensibility of form that enable us to recognise any image; and (at the *micro* level) that code of marks, lines, dots, and zones out of which an image is assembled. Each print process has certain visual characteristics, but the code of any one may be borrowed from or imitated by another.

Pictorial conventions must at some point (other than neurological response) be learnt, and so have a complex cultural character; they are also (since they are the ground rules of any visual representation) the visual forms of theories of knowledge. A study of the pictorial conventions surrounding the advent of the industrial system should reveal something of its cultural character and shed light on the construction of knowledge and our relation to the past through that construction.

The writer in the *Economist* assumed that the pictorial conventions of his day were 'a universal language' and that pictures 'as they approach perfection [are] equivalent . . . to seeing the objects themselves'. What did the writer mean by 'perfection'?

William Ivins, in his pioneer study of printed imagery, regards the pursuit of 'subliminality' as the driving factor in the evolution of the different processes.[14] Here I equate Ivins's subliminality with the 'perfection' demanded by the *Economist*, and with the use of 'subliminality' in information theory, by which the code does not appear in the message as 'noise'. The writer of 1851 was, in effect, demanding an invisible *means*, which would render the object of the picture 'perfectly'. Considered philosophically, this is a naïve empiricism; but considered ideologically it is a powerful demand for a 'neutral' or 'universal' visual code, close to the neurological process of vision, and which assumes a passive recipient subject. This naïve empiricism is the dominant pictorial convention of all early stages of industrial development. It drives out local visual culture as surely as Manchester printed cottons drove out vernacular textiles. Far from being a 'universal language' it is highly specific.

Ivins interprets the initial appeal of photography as due to its lack of what he calls 'syntax' – that is, an ordered and visible *code*. Areas of tone were not constructed by marks, but appeared by 'sun-painting', by 'the pencil of nature'. Though this is a concept of photography rejected in contemporary theory, within the limited possibilities of the 1840s such a conception could easily arise and easily become the dominant (because ideologically required) model of 'perfection'. Though the matter is immensely complicated, for the purposes of this study I mean to distinguish between those codes (approaching

14. Ivins, W. *Prints and Visual Communication* (Cambridge, Mass, MIT Press 1953). See also Jussim (1974).

'perfect' subliminality) which reinforce the reality of the pictured object – and of these, photography was predominant – and those codes that reinforce the reality of the viewing subject and the materiality of the picture surface (the painter's 'touch', the materiality of ink and bare paper – in a word, the 'faktura' of the image).

It is only through the first kind that any 'unmediated' experience can seem to be conveyed; it is therefore the mode of visualisation appropriate to that supposedly direct confrontation with the past that has been identified as one of the components of the 'heritage experience'. It presents its objects as 'given' rather than as 'constructed'. Its three-dimensional equivalent is the simulacrum, whose development we examine below.

The invention of so many different means of image reproduction brought with it a multiplicity of visual codes, many of which were used to imitative effect. Thus the aquatint reproduced the watercolour wash, the mezzotint the oil painter's chiaroscuro, the woodblock was forced to imitate the photograph and the photograph attempted to look like an etching. At length the halftone block combined the mezzotint and the photograph. All could be promiscuously mixed by lithography and its derivatives. The manipulation of images and the codes of their processes continues unabated down to the present day. To this has been added a popular understanding of visual conventions that had hitherto been the province of the specialist – diagrams, charts, technical drawings and similar previously arcane devices are now easily accepted.[15]

Thus the 'image explosion' is accompanied with an everaugmenting visual acuity and comprehensive understanding of visual codes, far in advance of any other epoch, and a very greatly extended range of visual conventions. There is no sign of this process coming to a halt. Indeed, the visual code discrimination of each generation, and the happy acceptance of new conventions, always appears to exceed that of the last. The capacity to absorb new visual conventions, and with them ideological shifts, is one of the necessary conditions of the continual expansion of 'the society of the spectacle'.

Occasions

A full study of the use and function of this image-mass would concern itself with studies of readership and match these with means, visual codes and conventions in some complicated matrix. This would then present a further set of problems, because the degree to which one could generalise from what is already a very general picture of English experience to that experienced in Ireland, (not to mention further afield) would be immensely problematic. But the excruciating

15. In 1813 John Smeaton found it necessary to explain that his technical drawings were 'little more than geometric lines, drawn to explain geometric and mechanical subjects. If any of them put on the appearance of anything further, it is to render it more explanatory and descriptive. They are, in reality, not meant as pictures . . .'. See Brett (1986).

difficulties ought not to prevent us attempting *some* account. We are dealing with one of the major episodes in the history of communications and the construction of knowledge.

To the *Economist* the essential function of the explosion was simply 'the diffusion of knowledge' by means independent of language or nationality. The illustrated periodical, the serial encyclopaedia, the manual of instruction were the visual counterparts of new literacy, new schools, mechanics institutes and schools of design. The titles explain themselves: *The Mirror of Literature, Amusement and Instruction* (1822), *The Library of Entertaining Knowledge* (1830), *The Penny Magazine* (backed by the Society for the Diffusion of Useful Knowledge) (1832) and *The Printing Machine: a review for the many* (1834).

Of course, these publications (and the many others like them) were not universal or neutral disseminators of knowledge. They were the communications system of a new order of society, of industrial capitalism in general; and where subordinate communities were concerned, the bearers of 'catastrophic' change. They represented a hegemony that was both ideological and visual, imposing new patterns of thought and response over older patterns.

Though this lies outside the main interest of our present study, the imposition of certain kinds of literacy and visual acuity by means of national schools and imported publications meant, in Ireland (as in anywhere else further away from the hegemonic 'centre'), a process of re-education out of customary means of communication and of construing the world. Previous conventions, previous means – oral traditions, early pictorial conventions and iconography – are constantly replaced by the new symbolic forms. And this would be true whatever their ostensible content.

The Penny Magazine and other publications organised by Charles Knight have been described as 'thinly disguised propaganda for Whig reform and economic policy'.[16] They contained précis of and commentaries upon Adam Smith and Andrew Ure's *Philosophy of Manufactures*. The *Illustrated London News* was one of the magazines that did *not* publish the vivid illustrations to the Parliamentary Reports on the Employment of Children in the Mines and Manufactures (May 1842).[17] *Bell's Penny Dispatch* however ran several pages (on 15 May 1842) of illustrations of harnessed and naked children, and precipitated political action. The age of the image-essay and of visual propaganda had begun in earnest. (For further comment on this, *see* chapter 5.)

The Penny Magazine was also influential in the dissemination of artistic education. Edward Cowper's evidence to the 1835–6 Parliamentary Enquiry into Arts and Manufactures gives a clear picture both of the scale and the manner of image distribution:

16. Fox, C. 'Graphic Journalism in England in the 1830s and 1840s', unpublished doctoral thesis; University of Oxford (1974), p. 145.

17. For discussion, see ch. 5 and the Strokestown Famine Museum.

Here you may see it exemplified in *The Penny Magazine* . . . many taken from the old masters, of painting and sculpture, and many of them very well done; and these 150 cuts, printed on drawing paper and well bound, may be had for 14s. Such works as this and *The Saturday Magazine, Chamber's Journal* and the *Magasin Pittoresque* and the *Magasin Universel de Paris* could not have existed without the printing machine . . . every Saturday 360,000 copies of these useful publications are issued to the public . . .

596. And is not this means of diffusing a knowledge of the arts (not by bringing people to places of instruction in art, but by conveying instruction to the doors of the people) a new era of instruction in design? – Decidedly . . . it is quite clear that there are hundreds of thousands of people who are now acquainted . . . that would never have known them by any lecture of description whatever, and who would never have an opportunity of seeing the originals.[18]

18. British Parliamentary Papers (Irish University Press Series, Shannon, Irish UP, 17 June 1836).

This was the creation of mass taste, and so thorough was the work that mass taste has altered very little since. It was also the assembly of a widely distributed body of information, apparently neutral, in the form of an 'image bank' of stock conventions from which concepts such as 'heritage' could later be distilled.

Whatever the intended or ostensible function of these illustrated journals and albums may have been, they all had more in common than in contradiction. That commonality is a definition of a social reality. Information, knowledge and taste are defined as entities of such a kind that they can be 'diffused', extended and made available by explicit visual imagery. This demanded a type of imagery with 'high-fact-content', with a subliminal code that reinforced the reality of the pictured object. In certain cases, social reality was seen to be identical with information flow: in a final self-congratulatory address, the Society for the Diffusion of Useful Knowledge closed itself down with the thought that 'The time is coming . . . when the Society . . . shall be co-extensive with society itself.'[19] The first editorial of the *Illustrated London News* proclaimed (on 14 May 1842) that 'There is now no staying the advance of [illustration] into all the departments of our social system . . . We sail into the very heart and focus of public life.'

19. See Smith, H. *The Society for the Diffusion of Useful Knowledge 1826–1846: a social and bibliographical evaluation* (Halifax, Nova Scotia 1974), p. 100.

The commercial usage of this image-mass followed, with some exceptions, the informational and educational use; but the three are closely linked. Information, knowledge and taste were diffused, extended and made accessible as if they were commodities; thus a commercial usage of imagery followed naturally.

Although advertising as a business was well established in the 1830s, the material was primarily textual and typographic. Illustration, when used, was simply iconic, presenting an image of the goods to be sold as in a shop sign. An hypothesis worth investigating would be this – that modern advertising owes its origins to the relations between text and image first established in the pages of journals such as the *Illustrated London News*, to the habit of reading image and text as one experience. A study of the extension of pictorial advertising, whilst clearly a part of the overall topic, has to be foregone, for reasons of brevity.

I have outlined the growth of what Peter Fuller has described as the 'megavisual tradition', which the *Economist* first identified in 1851.[20] This image-saturated culture seems to be inseparable from the consuming function of the industrial system.

> Open any glossy magazine and you will see merchandise as a fetish. The product of the machine has become the cult image of our society. Where, then, should we expect to find the artist in our society. Where he was before, where the myths are made, and there he is, in the advertising agencies, in the dream factories of the consumer society.[21]

This process (first described by Marx in chapter 5 of *Capital*, on the fetishisation of commodities) involves imagery in the stimulation and sustaining of demand; and amongst those demands is the apprehension of the past, unmediated and 'subliminal'. The spectacular, even phantasmagorical character of our apprehension of social (and therefore historical) reality begins here in the early image explosion, and has fed upon the multiplication of imagery ever since.

20. Fuller, P. *Beyond the Crisis in Art* (London, Writers and Readers Co-operative 1980), p. 53.

21. Del Renzio, T. 'Art is Modern, Bourgeois, Conceptual and Marginal' in *Art for Society* (London, Whitechapel Art Gallery catalogue 1978).

II: The Spectacle

This strictly two-dimensional 'image explosion' developed in parallel with a great range of visual and spectacular entertainments and events, with which it was closely enmeshed. This was centred around phenomena such as panoramas, and reaches its climax in the series of Great Exhibitions held throughout Europe and the Americas in the later part of the century. These exhibitions have, of course, continued; but the visual entertainments of wide-screen and 'multi-media' spectacles, complete with music and special effects, have now been almost entirely absorbed into the film and television industries, whose parents they are.

The Great Exhibition of 1851 has always been regarded, with good reason, as the 'point of departure' for the project of modernism (no matter how conceived). Where heritage is concerned, the exhibition, with its 'medieval court' and its displays according to national origin, marks a point in the development of tourism-in-time. Where actual tourism is concerned (and here 'heritage' is included as an element in tourist entertainment), 1851 conveniently marks the date of the 'package holiday'. The amassing of objects was accompanied by an amassing of people.

Special cheap entrance tickets were instituted (Monday to Thursday) and abridged guidebooks and catalogues were on sale. Of the six million recorded visitors, more than four million were the so-called 'shilling people'. The railways offered cheap return fares with the aim of attracting the working population from the provinces; very large numbers of foreign visitors were recorded. Around these masses a tourist trade developed in central London, which included (in addition to catering and accommodation) the provision of imagery and spectacle.[22]

22. Rosner, C. *A Printer's Progress* (London 1951) contains much relevant material. Christopher Hobhouse's book *1851 and the Great Exhibition* remains a very useful study. See also Greenhalgh (below) and Brett (1984).

The image of the Crystal Palace was printed, stamped or moulded onto every surface that could bear a picture. Souvenirs, albums, picture-books, models, songsheets, clothing, wallpaper and letter-heads carried its picture all around Europe and beyond. Illustrators caricatured or described all national costumes and racial types. A gift book – *The House that Caxton Built* (6d., coloured) – shows all the races of humankind upon the cover, and a *Parlour Magazine for the Literature of All Nations* was published and on sale within the building. Out in the town, according to *The Times* of 21 Aug. 1851, there were no less than nine panoramas or dioramas on display, plus one vast model of the globe.

The vistas to be seen were of all the European cities, the Hellespont, Niagara Falls, and the sights to be seen on the overland journey to India culminating in a view of the Taj Mahal. They represented, in the midst of real tourism, a virtual or vicarious form of 'pictorial conveyance'. Their association with the Great Exhibition was not fortuitous, since the exhibition was conceived in terms of a 'panoramic' conspectus of human ingenuity.

It is in the concept of packaging that objects and images meet. Just as the exhibition contained machines for wrapping up goods for consumption, so there was an industry to 'wrap up' the world in pictorial form. Until this time, both real and vicarious tourism had been as scarce and expensive as the hand-crafted imagery to which it was related, through the picturesque and the sublime; but from 1851 it becomes possible to speak of the growth of world tourism, and reality as spectacle. With spectacle comes the simulacrum, and the complicated skills of simulation. The creation of the panoramic display predates significantly the development of large international exhibitions, and the rhetoric of these exhibitions does in fact depend upon that already developed by the visual entertainment industry that condensed around Robert Barker's invention.

The panorama and its many variants were the predominant visual entertainment of the early to mid-nineteenth century, only finally dying out with the advent of cinema, which replaced them. The impact of these shows upon the broader visual culture of the century, and upon the growth of new forms of popular under-standings (including popular history), is without doubt important, though difficult to quantify.

Most early panoramas were essentially a gigantic extension from the picturesque principle of the favoured viewpoint or 'station', and were mainly topographical – an all-embracing view of the city being the most common; though views from mountain tops were also favoured, as were scenes of naval and land battles. The relation between these spectacles and the 'fine' art of the landscape painter is a very interesting subject with which we have no time to grapple. They were presented to the public in terms that were a mixture of showmanship, artistic promotion and educational value.

The first major public example is from 1791, when Robert Barker and Son presented a series of shows in Leicester Square, London, based on a patent of 1787. Barker was an Irish artist working in Edinburgh, who conceived of the idea for essentially artistic reasons, but soon realised its commercial potential: 'While Robert Barker's idea of 360° painting had a certain novelty value, it was his concep-tion of the painting as a large-scale exhibition mimicking nature that was his most original and influential contribution.'[23]

In its typical form, the panorama was housed in a circular build-ing and viewed from a central platform; careful lighting (derived from stage lamps) was planned to illuminate the painted surface just sufficiently to reveal the image without revealing its painted character; it was thus meant to be experienced as a 'perfect' and subliminal simulation rather than as a painting on canvas. Barker believed that he had made 'an Improvement on Painting, which relieves that sublime Art from a Restraint it has ever laboured under'. 'It appeared to those overcome by the panorama's effects that a new age of verisimilitude in painting was being ushered in.'[24] One visitor reported:

> I have been to see Mr. Barker's panoramas, the Siege of Flushing, and the Bay of Messina. They are so well painted as to be quite decep-tion . . . as they extend in a circular form all round the rooms and the spectators are placed in the centre the effect is very astonishing. I actually put on my hat imagining myself to be in the open air. These pictures exhibit both branches of perspective in perfection, for I was so far deceived that I could form no idea how far the canvas was from my eye, in one spot it appears thirty miles off and in another not so many feet, such is the astonishing effect that can be produced by a strict adherence to Nature.[25]

23. Hyde, R. *Panoramania: the Art and Entertainment of the All-embracing View* (London, Trefoil Publications in assoc. with The Barbican Gallery 1988), p. 17. And see also Sobieszek, R. (ed.) *The Prehistory of Photography; Five Texts* (New York, Arno Press New York 1979), and Lawson, T. 'Time Vampires, Space Bandits', in *Artforum*, 5, 26 Jan. 1988.

24. Hyde, op. cit., p. 25.

25. Ibid., p. 38. The notion of nature is interesting here, being subordinated to the conventions of its depiction. In the sense developed above, the commentator surely means 'perfect' or 'subliminal' rendering so as to give 'immediate' effect.

Barker's original idea was modified by his successors; amongst the most remarkable was the 'moving panorama' which consisted of a viewing room or hall (often a small theatre or lecture hall was employed) which contained a proscenium arch and suffcient back-stage space to house the cylinders on which the image was held. The image – usually painted on linen – was unrolled by cranks and handles across the stage space onto a second cylinder, much as in the winding mechanism of a camera. There was appropriate lighting (early gas and electric arc filaments were very quickly put into theatrical service) and there was a musical accompaniment provided either by a small band, a piano, or a mechanical instrument. There was often a narrator or lecturer who gave a spoken commentary. Special mechanical and other effects were increasingly introduced, which pushed the panorama concept further away from painting and increasingly toward what we would now describe as a multi-media simulation.

Some of these moving panorama were of great size and represented a considerable capital outlay which had to be recouped by taking the spectacle on tour. Some of the grandest were American. 'Whaling Around the World' was painted on a continuous cloth 8 feet 6 inches high and 1,275 feet long. Designed by Benjamin Russell and Caleb Purvington in 1847, it toured the United States, arriving and ending in New York in 1851: it portrayed a journey round the globe in search of whales, with visits to exotic places.[26] Another very large production (claiming to be three miles in length) was John Banvard's 'Great Panorama of the Mississippi River' (1846) which, after a five-year tour, arrived in London in 1851 and was visited by Queen Victoria. British panoramas seem to have been generally on a smaller scale, but more expertly produced. A notable example was 'The Ascent of Mont Blanc' seen at the Egyptian Hall in Piccadilly, and illustrated in the *Illustrated London News* for 25 December 1852. Amongst other topics recorded we find visits to Pompeii, the full story of the *Pilgrim's Progress*, episodes from *Paradise Lost* and scenes from the Napoleonic Wars (with the Battle of Waterloo the most popular). Travels in the Alps, to Constantinople and to Paris were hardy favourites, as well as Oriental tours as noted above. In the United States, the Civil War (after its end) proved another important subject. All over Europe similar shows were created; panorama buildings appeared in all the major cities, and successful works were taken on continental tours. Napoleon Bonaparte, recognising the powerful propaganda possibilities of the medium, had eight rotundas planned for the Champs-Elysées to show the great struggles of the revolution and his battles.

26. See Avery, K.J. 'Whaling Around the World', in *The American Art Journal* 22, 1, pp. 50 *et seq*. The paint cloth has been preserved – a monument of popular graphic art. It seems possible that Hermann Melville knew the panorama whilst writing *Moby Dick*.

As might be expected, the artists most concerned in the creation of panoramas and their variants were professionally connected on the one hand with the picturesque tradition of topographical painting, and on the other hand with theatre scenery and architecture. Thomas Girtin was particularly prominent; his 'Great Picture of London' or the 'Eidometropolis' seems (on the evidence of existing sketches in the British Museum) to have been exceptionally fine. It was described in the *Monthly Magazine* (October 1802) as the 'connoisseur's panorama'; after Girtin's early death it was bought by a Russian nobleman and exhibited in St Petersburg. John Knox showed a 'Grand Painting of the View from Ben Lomond' in a rotunda on The Mound, Edinburgh, in 1811. Frederick Catherwood and David Roberts, who had applied picturesque practice to the Middle East as 'Orientalist' artists, were responsible for increasingly sublime views such as 'The Israelites Leaving Egypt' (1829) and 'The Temple of Baalbek' (1833) (actually an enlargement of a much smaller easel painting that is now in Birmingham). In the sublime mode, John Martin's painting *Belshazzars Feast* (1820) was enlarged and copied by Louis Daguerre's assistant Hippolyte Sebron, and shown in London in 1833 and later in New York. In Berlin, K.F. Schinkel, before he won renown as an architect, created a series of elaborate displays or 'optical perspectives' that included transparencies, back and front lighting, musical accompaniment and incorporated movement (1807–11). The involvement of architects, particularly the Pugin family, in these displays establishes an important link between the representation of the past as entertainment, and its re-creation in built form. We can speculate that Pugin *fils* was attempting to realise, in the actual world of the 1840s, the virtual reality that he and his father had been creating in the 1830s.[27]

Perhaps most significant of all was the photographer-to-be Louis Daguerre who opened dioramas in specially prepared buildings in both Paris and London (1822 and 1823). The London building was constructed in Regent's Park and designed by A.C. Pugin; it was equipped with the latest technical devices and lighting and continued in business until 1851.[28] Daguerre's interest in the technology of representation, established in his work for theatres and dioramas, led directly toward the development of photography and, what is perhaps more important, the commercial exploitation of the new invention.

Ralph Hyde has summed up the appeal of the panorama in terms exactly appropriate to our enquiry:

> The panorama supplied a substitute for travel and a supplement to the newspaper . . . when in 1842 a new publication married printed word to visual image in the form of the *Illustrated London News*, the panorama had already been providing a pictorial documentation of current events and places of interest for over half a century.[29]

27. For a description of the Pugin family involvement in theatre etc., see Lionel Lambourne's 'Pugin and the Theatre' in Atterbury P. and Wainwright C. *Pugin; a Gothic Passion* (London, Yale U. Press and the Victoria and Albert Museum 1994).

28. For an account of Daguerre's work in this field, see Potonniee, G. 'Daguerre: Peintre et Decorateur', in Sobieszek (1979).

29. Hyde, op. cit., p. 38.

The idea of the panoramic view was extended by analogy into every field of knowledge. The *News* itself declared that its aim was 'to keep continually before the eye of the world a living and moving panorama of all its actions and influences' and the form was held to be, in some respects, more educationally valuable than an actual visit to the places depicted. Charles Dickens's character, Mr Booley, portrays himself travelling the entire globe in his retirement by means of 'the gigantic-moving-panorama or diorama mode of conveyance which I have principally adopted (all my modes of conveyance have been pictorial)'.[30]

30. From 'Household Words' (1850) quoted by Hyde, p. 38.

Further developments of the panorama concept were toward portability or greater complexity. Peepshows and optical toys, stereoscopic viewers and booths were developed, with both entertaining and instructive intentions. 'Cosmoramas' and 'kineoramas' appear, with moving parts, as do increasingly ambitious stage effects; later in the century 'cycloramas' and 'electroramas' were created by multiple projections. The globe advertised in *The Times* in 1851 (*see* above) was a spherical building through which the public passed on iron gantries to view a range of images. Special railway carriages were designed to accommodate other spectacles. Photographic panoramas and segmented photographs of great size are recorded from the 1850s onward. A more complete study of this progressive 'visualisation' would include discussion of small-scale and domestic devices such as 'shadowgraphs', magic lantern displays, 'zoetropes', 'stereoscopes', 'cartes megalographiques', 'protean views', kaleidoscopes and a whole range of peepshows and toy theatres.[31]

31. An excellent account of these inventions will be found in the Barnes Museum of Cinematography, St Ives, Cornwall, whose catalogue *Precursors of the Cinema* (1967) is useful.

There is good evidence to suppose that the panoramas and visual toys were originally aimed at a middle-class audience, but that as the century progressed they became increasingly 'popular'. How this relates to the increase of real, rather than pictorial travel, remains to be researched.

> To those who would never see the real locations, panorama images were a surrogate reality, against which other representations, either verbal or pictorial, could be weighed. To those who would later visit the sites represented, the panorama image provided a framework for the actual experience of reality.[32]

32. Hyde, op. cit., p. 40.

However, a very significant number of the recorded shows were of historical, and often national/historical subjects. There is no doubt that the multi-media heritage displays of today are the direct descendants of these early nineteenth-century spectacles, and that they combined both the functions of entertainment and instruction in presenting the national past.

These two-dimensional panoramas were accompanied by three-dimensional simulations, most notably in special sections of the great exhibitions. The exhibition of 1851 contained, for example, 'The Medieval Court', in which an array of neo-Gothic manufactures were assembled in a special neo-Gothic enclave. There was also an Oriental court in which the textiles and metalwork of India were displayed – these were, in point of fact, goods specially commissioned by the East India Company for the European market and rather than being 'authentically Indian', they bodied forth a particular concept of 'the Orient' that appealed to contemporary taste. A whole Caribbean hut was obtained and re-erected in the Crystal Palace as an example of native architecture.[33]

Subsequent international exhibitions developed these enclaves by importing not artefacts but human beings, usually in the form of a 'native village'. These have recently been studied in some detail by Paul Greenhalgh and by Annie Coombes:

> Brought from all areas of the . . . empire, groups of people would be settled into an appropriate surrounding where they would live, night and day, for the six months of the exposition. Often they were given the materials to build their own dwellings and invariably they were supplied with foodstuffs and raw material to prepare their own meals and make their own clothes. They would usually be situated near other 'native villages' on the site, they would be expected to perform religious rituals at set times each day for the visitors and to give demonstrations of their various arts and crafts.[34]

Egyptian bazaars, Tunisian barber shops and Algerian cafés were open for business beside Senegalese or Dahomeyan huts. Nubian, Eskimo, Lapp, Gaucho, Kalmuck, North American Indian, Ceylonese, New Caledonian, Gabonese, Ashanti, and Javan and Maori groups are recorded. The Paris Exposition of 1889 took this ethnographic imperialism most seriously:

> A popular feature of the show is the street, not of an ancient civilised city, but of aboriginal savages. In the back settlements behind all the gorgeous finery of the pagoda and the palaces of the further East, the ingenious French have established colonies of savages whom they are attempting to civilize. They are the genuine article and make no mistake, living and working and amusing themselves as they and their kinfolk do in their country. Some day an enthusiast promises us we shall have a great anthropological exhibition of living samples of all nations and tribes and peoples that on earth do dwell. That may be the next Universal Exhibition.[35]

It is hardly possible to consider these spectacles today without a mortifying sense of shame, but they were very popular. They

33. This hut, as studied by Gottfried Semper, became the principal example in his theory of craft and architecture, and thus a starting point for a great deal of twentieth-century culture!

34. See Greenhalgh, P. *Ephemeral Vistas: The Expositions Universelles, Great Exhibitions and World Fairs 1851–1939* (Manchester UP 1988), p. 83. I am generally indebted to Greenhalgh in this section. See also Coombes, A.E. 'Ethnography and the Foundation of National and Cultural Perspectives', in Hiller, S. (ed.) *The Myth of Primitivism: Perspectives on Art* (London, Routledge, 1991).

35. Ibid., p. 88.

served several significant ideological functions, of which the imperial was merely the most obvious. They provided evidence for the crass 'social Darwinism' that was used to justify expansion, and they helped to construct a racism that overflowed the boundaries of normal class or national conflict. Particular 'villages' were, in fact, toured from one exhibition to another, across national borders, rather like circuses. (And the contemporary reader should bear in mind that these phenomena are by no means extinct; though today they are presented as 'ethnic' entertainment.)

But these human showcases were not invariably of the exotic and the conquered. They served as advertisements for the character and the history of the participating nations, and for their goods. There are many examples of 'white' villages: Belgian, English, German, Austrian, Swedish and Dutch villages were especially popular in the United States. These were, it seems without exception, highly idealised exercises in a 'picturesque' vernacular style; the English villages were complete with Maypoles and greens. The emphasis was upon rural values supposedly rooted in tradition, language and local custom: 'Most nations showed themselves as residing in pleasant holiday camps, where everybody had plenty, everyone was content, and everyone knew his or her folk-tunes by heart.'[36]

36. Ibid., p. 106.

Accompanying these villages, there were frequent displays of city life 'from the past'. According to Greenhalgh, the Austrians were the first, creating an 'old Vienna' as part of a large exhibition in 1873, but subsequently we find 'old London' 'old Paris' and even 'old New York' making appearances. The 'old Paris' of 1900 was an immensely successful and immensely expensive simulation of a medieval *quartier*, filled with hundreds of 'extras' in medieval garb walking its streets.

To display oneself abroad was one thing, to do so at home was quite another, and here the propaganda function of the village and its picturesque mode of simulation becomes much more evident. The Irish village of Ballymaclinton was a large feature of the Franco–British exhibition of 1908, and it was retained for three successive exhibitions at White City. It was accompanied by a Scottish village in 1909. The 1908 exhibition was itself a propaganda exercise relating to the Entente Cordiale, but within that frame it is quite clear that the Irish exhibit served a function of normalising the image of Ireland at a moment when Home Rule agitation and Ulster insurgency were dominating British politics.

> Ballymaclinton presented Ireland as ancient and rural, with thatched cottages, peat-burners, traditional dancing and the Gaelic language; all was wrapped in a self-sufficiency scarcely less complete than that of the Senegalese Village next to it.[37]

37. Ibid., p. 107.

Coombes sets Ballymaclinton against the development, in both anthropological and political circles, of a concept of 'national culture' and plans for museums that would demonstrate its existence. Henry Balfour, president of the Anthropological Institute, declared in 1904 that

> We want a National Museum . . . National in the sense that it deals with the people of the British Isles, their arts, their industries, customs and beliefs, local differences in physical and cultural characteristics, the development of appliances, the survival of primitive forms in certain districts, and so forth.[38]

38. Quoted in Coombes, op. cit., p. 205.

Such a concept was at work in exhibition design before it found its way into permanent museum collections. Thus Irish and Scottish villages are constituted as 'intra-British primitive' and defined as part of a national culture through what Coombes describes as 'the discourse of origination'.

That Ireland had been one of the pioneers of major exhibitions, with the Dublin Exhibition of 1853, was forgotten in the urge to redraw the cultural map of the British Isles. It is entirely of a piece with this elision, that the Scottish village was represented as a Highland idyll (despite the fact that Scotland was the engine-room of the entire imperial project).

Greenhalgh presents these Irish and Scottish villages as exemplars of the 'core–periphery' phenomenon. The Celtic regions had to be differentiated and primitivised

> [I]n order for the English to be able to differentiate themselves and rule . . . the emphasis on the Celtic and Gaelic languages in some exhibitions had the effect of further emphasising their 'otherness' . . . [but] . . . When the English presented their own Tudor village, as they often did in America, an entirely different set of values were brought to bear; their rurality was not to do with backwardness or indolence, but with tradition and stability in the face of industrial change.[39]

39. Greenhalgh, op. cit., pp. 107–8.

However, as with the case of Irish landscape painting and the discourse of the picturesque, discussed in the previous chapter, the 'national village' idea is not by any means so simple as exemplar as Greenhalgh suggests, because the 'periphery' can itself assimilate and internalise the description it has received from the 'core'. Something of this can be seen at work in the Scottish Exhibition of National History, Art and Industry held in Glasgow in 1911.[40] In this exhibition, which was conceived and organised by Glaswegians, the historical emphasis was strong; one aim of the exhibition was to endow a chair of Scottish History at University of Glasgow and there was a (temporary) Palace of History, housing an immense

40. This short account is indebted to Kinchin, P. and Kinchin, J. *Glasgow's Great Exhibitions 1888, 1901, 1911, 1939, 1988* (Bicester, White Cockade Press 1992).

collection of relics to 'call up memories of kings and peasants, peace and war' (the catalogue ran to 1,155 pages). The display of authentic objects was believed to lead to the 'vivification' of the national past. There was also an 'Auld Toon' which included a castle keep and a 'Typical Scottish Town Hall'; this 'Toon' was described as a 'quiet, old-world nook, with its towering turrets . . . a place apart, a sport to which one may retire from the din and ecstasy of the coming summer nights and recall the picturesque and historic past'. As P. and J. Kinchin have pointed out, 'This consumer-oriented, trim and tidy "living history" concept has proved enormously successful in the twentieth century.'[41] The 'Auld Toon' was inhabited by appropriately clad persons; and there were historical pageants.

41. See Kinchin and Kinchin op. cit., p. 103.

Also in Glasgow, in addition to the (by now customary) 'African village', and a Lapp encampment, there was 'An Clachan' – a Highland village conceived with

> the patriotic object of arousing a greater interest in the Highland people, in their traditions and customs, in their beautiful Gaelic language, literature and music, in their distinctive Celtic art, and especially to afford a unique opportunity for exhibiting and disposing the Highland Home Industries to the vast concourse of people who will visit the Exhibition from many lands.[42]

42. Ibid., p. 122.

Postcards of An Clachan have the background of Glasgow's modern buildings skilfully brushed away.

This exhibition was perhaps one of the most 'heritage-directed' events of its kind in that period, and would reward close study. Its promotion and success appear to be linked to the growing decline of Glaswegian industry and to the progressive loss of financial autonomy; its character may be compared with the modernist and international tone of the 1901 exhibition on the same site.[43]

As the twentieth century progressed, international exhibitions became the venues for intensely propagandistic displays. The political rivalries of right and left were fought out in visual terms. Italian fascism, more than any other movement, relied upon the power of spectacle.

43. See Brett, D. *C.R. Mackintosh: The Poetics of Workmanship* (London, Reaktion Books 1992), p. 130 and Eadie, W. *Movements of Modernity; the Case of Glasgow and Art Nouveau* (London, Routledge 1990), pp. 232–3.

44. Schnapp, J. T. 'Epic Demonstrations: Fascist Modernity and the 1932 Exhibition of the Fascist Revolution', in *Fascism, Aesthetics and Culture*, R.J. Golsan (ed.) (Hanover NH. University Press of New England 1992), p. 3. Schnapp takes the reader on a fascinating 'narrative' through this exhibition, similar to that which I attempt in the next chapter.

> Unlike communism, its enemy twin, fascism, could not settle the question of its identity via recourse to the utopias of science and/or theory (no matter how resolutely it sometimes strove to do so). Rather, fascism required an aesthetic overproduction – a surfeit of fascist signs, images, slogans, books and buildings – to compensate for, fill in, and cover up its forever unstable ideological core.[44]

Part of this 'overproduction' was conceived in heritage terms; Mussolini seems to have been one of the first political figures to use the term in a modern sense. 'We mustn't simply exploit our cultural heritage' he declared in 1926, 'we must create a new heritage to place alongside that of antiquity.'[45]

There is a final element in the 'technology of representation' that requires some mention, since it figures largely (and often bathetically) in displays of heritage; I mean simulated human beings in the form of dummies, static or animated.

There is a long history of automata and mechanical women and men, but more relevant is the development of the waxwork museum. This is identified in the contemporary mind with Madame Tussaud, but her remarkable business, dating back to the 1780s, was by no means the only one. Wax simulacra had long been in use as an aid to the teaching of anatomy, before they were turned to the purposes of mass entertainment. J.C. Curtius's 'Caverne des Grandes Voleurs' (1783) in Paris seems to have been the best early example – filled with the portraits of notorious villains. The skills of the establishment were called upon, during the revolutionary period, to model the features of its martyrs and victims – notably the assassinated Marat. Such images are reported to have been paraded about the city, in processions. Mme Tussaud herself – a skilled partner – is said to have found herself modelling the severed head of one of her former patrons, as well as the head of Robespierre. In 1802, during the Peace of Amiens, Tussaud fled to London, bringing with her most of Curtius's stock of figures; setting up in the Strand, the high quality of her exhibits soon eclipsed all rivals. Here she initiated a policy that helped to create the concept of 'celebrity'. 'If the hour brought with it a Man, or a Woman, famous or infamous, the personage of that Hour was forthwith modelled, coloured, dressed, and given a place in the Baker Street Galleries.'[46] However, the main part of her constantly changing exhibition was always composed of a mix of recent and national/historical figures, comparable in their own terms with the subjects shown in panoramas.[47] The changing display shows a slow progress away from popular history, toward contemporary record and 'celebrity'.

What is most interesting about Tussaud's and other waxwork displays – apart from the balance of their subject matter – is the character of the images and their materials. Wax is, of all commonly available substances, the one that most readily simulates living tissue; to which is added the real (i.e. non-metaphorical) use of clothing and other items. The waxwork seems to have answered to the same demand as the all-enclosing panorama and, later, as the photograph and the 'human showcase' – that of presenting what appeared to be a 'perfect' (in Ivins's terms, 'noise-less' or subliminal) rendition of a person or human situation, 'a surrogate reality against which other representations, verbal or pictorial, could be weighed'.

45. 'Arte e civiltà' in *Opera Omnia* Florence 1951–63, 22, p. 230, quoted by Schnapp.

46. *Madame Tussaud's Exhibition Guide and Catalogue, 1937.*

47. The mix of figures in 1937, for example, was of 'Famous Soldiers and Sailors' (11), the royal family (17), the cabinet and other politicians (34), American presidents (12), religious figures from the national past (18), foreign heads of state (12), famous authors (15), record-breakers and other famous persons (19), personalities of various kinds (55), kings and queens of England (only) (58), murderers etc. (29) and a handful of others including Voltaire, 'a coquette', Richard Wagner and the king of Bulgaria (19); finally a series of tableaux including 'The Death of Nelson', 'The Granting of Magna Carta' and 'An Arena in Ancient Rome' (12).

48. Boorstin, D. *The Image; A Guide to Pseudo-events in America* (New York, Vintage Books 1992, first edn. 1961), p. 103.

In his survey of 'pseudo-events', Boorstin treats of waxworks (along with other tourist attractions) as 'of little significance for the inward life of a people'.[48] This seems to me an entirely misconceived criticism; insofar as a 'people' have an 'inward life' (and his organicist analogy is revealing of his own political stance), it is constituted by and from shared representations, and during the early nineteenth century the waxwork museum established itself as a significant former of these representations (which role it has never wholly lost). It did so, because its means, conventions and occasions were part of the visual ideology of the time – which industrial society still maintains, though not with the same means and exclusivity.

Subsequently, and by steps that need not concern us, there was an interbreeding between the static waxworks and the mechanised automata, whereby 'animatronic' descendants have been bred from the original stock.

The modes of visualisation and simulation, considered both as techniques and as symbolic forms, prepared the way for the visual presentation of popular history. They are predominating features of industrial and post-industrial culture, and a necessary condition for the construction of heritage.

5

TOWARD A CRITICAL METHOD

We are now at the moment in this study when we can begin to formulate a critical method whereby some classes of 'heritage' phenomena can be analysed and criticised. Such a method will, of course, be provisional; but, as I asserted in my introduction, it is better to have a provisional method than none at all. This is proposed so that others can replace it with better.

As I also asserted at the very start of this book, the study of heritage is self-evidently worthwhile; and not least because it is a contemporary form of popular history which cannot but be involved in pertinent questions about the nation, the state, the region, identity and culture. A critical method has to provide us with findings, positions, and possible readings that elucidate these questions.

Here we are concerned with built environments such as 'centres' 'interpretive buildings' and 'parks'; that is with large and tangible manifestations of the heritage idea that lend themselves to analysis based on visual and spatial concepts. I am proposing three main headings under which this method can proceed. They will not lend themselves so easily to other less physical displays, nor to the general use of the concept; but I believe they will contribute to making some of the problems involved in making any heritage display more comprehensible. I hope they will be useful to anyone ready to spend a little time and effort, as visitors, as commentators, and as creators of such displays.

The first two headings, of *visualisation* and *simulation,* have already been the subject of discussion. By the first I mean those modes of pictorial convention which are employed; such modes typically come under the general rubric of 'picturesque' and 'sublime', but there are others we might employ. For instance, we are now at the historical point at which a certain version of 'modernism' has come to seem part of 'heritage'; this is a matter we shall touch upon later.

By the second I mean the device of accurate replication in three-dimensional form, which may, of course, include real persons; and it also includes the simulation of sounds, tastes and smells. Most typically, in our context, it refers to those reconstructions of the past which attempt verisimilitude.

Before engaging with them, however, it is necessary to develop the third a little further; it has had a shadowy existence in the text so far and needs to be brought into clear focus before we proceed further. The third heading is *narrative topology*. Narrative topology is, briefly, the arrangement of spaces and the connections between them such that they set up, suggest or assert relationships between whatever is displayed in those spaces. The notion derives essentially from architecture, and what I mean by it is best illustrated through the circulation patterns and hierarchies of spaces in typical buildings.

A circulation pattern is created by the flow through halls, doors, courts and corridors: it can have many geometrical characteristics, but its function is to lead us into, through and out of the building in some appropriate manner. It is, in effect, the traffic system of a building, and of course in any planning of a major construction, the effect of its internal circulation has to take into account its effect upon the circulation outside. While much of this is merely practical – can we escape in a fire? – circulation patterns may also be highly symbolic or associative. We 'come down' the aisle, and 'approach' the magistrate's bench; we are 'led' into the great hall; we 'explore' the attics and the cellars. Much of the pleasures and excitements of a great building consist in a kind of progressive realisation of its spaces as we move through them in an ordered or mysterious sequence.

Not only that, circulation is a form of social ordering. The development of the corridor, for example, permitted the development of personal privacy in bedroom and study; the rooms opening off the hall (indeed, the very idea of the central hall) enables special activities (such as dining) to be held in special places. Formally distinct rooms both permit and develop formally distinct social functions (withdrawing, entertaining, even in the case of *le boudoir*, sulking). The formal separation of different social classes has often been expressed through separate passageways, stairs and entrances (see below for a discussion of Strokestown Park House). The removal of a wall between back and front rooms (so common today in terrace houses) is a simplification of circulation that abolishes different functions in response to changed *mores*. The difference between front and back entrances, and the very differentiation of 'front' and 'back' both express and form social manners through patterns of movement. Circulation is spatialised etiquette.

Circulation is also the link between spaces, and particularly between spaces of greater and lesser importance. The relative importance of different rooms and courtyards is established by many means – size, accessibility, splendour, special treatment, etc. The aim is to proclaim the function of a space and the importance of that function; examples do not need to be given. How spaces and places succeed one another, how they are entered and left, and the patterns of impression formed by their succeeding qualities are all capable of yielding meanings. What this means at the everyday level can be discovered by beginning with such innocent questions as 'Why am I being led in this direction?', or 'Why is this room so grand?' or (often an important query) 'Why is this entrance made so narrow?'

In an exhibition, the circulation pattern is part of the construction of a narrative: it says – come this way and see this and then this and then that. This ordering is likely to be part of an explanatory pattern, or historical sequence (typical examples of this abound in art galleries). It may also say – you can see anything you like in any order that is topologically feasible; and so abandon attempts at demonstrating causality. It may, or may not, provide for alternative narratives. As we shall see, a study of this narrative ordering is particularly important in determining the intentional structure of a display or a park.

In a purpose-built museum the different spaces can serve (or obstruct) the intellectual function of *categorisation*. They may do so by deliberate design, or (more likely) by the interplay between existing intellectual categories and the desire of museum curators to display their collections in harmony with the spaces that are available, but which can't easily be altered. The degree to which the building type moulds the emotional and intellectual experience it contains is a matter for subtle enquiry.

The original plan of the British Museum (now much enlarged and modified) was based upon the typical *palazzi* of Italy; it consisted essentially of an open square with sequences of rooms arranged around it linked by doors that opened directly from one room into another. Corridors were few and short and nearly all the building was easily accessible by simply passing from one room to another in one of two directions. The circular reading room was placed so as to be central yet secluded. The actual exhibition spaces opened up from and into one another directly, and were generally similar in size and character. Only the entrance and the stair-wells were specially distinct.

These spaces expressed, but also imposed, a pattern of categorisation. Each room had a topic ('Egyptian', 'Anglo-Saxon', 'Babylonian and Assyrian') or a class of artefact ('coins and medals', 'glass and ceramics'). The categories are, in fact, rather confused and we can imagine the difficulty curators must have experienced deciding appropriate sequences because the building, being a massive neo-classical structure, admits of no easy alteration. This general plan, with its difficulties, was common to most nineteenth-century museums.

In the twentieth century a more critical epistemology has suggested a more fluid disposition of space and circulation. Le Corbusier proposed a museum consisting of a steadily growing spiral

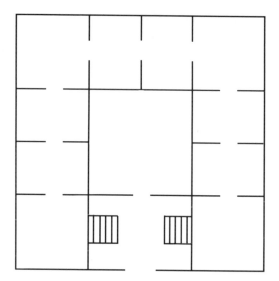

5.1: Typical nineteenth-
century museum plan,
based on earlier *palazzi.*

of interconnecting pavilions; but a fine counter-example is the
Pompidou Centre or Musée Beaubourg in Paris where several large
spaces with no permanent structures within them are stacked one
over the other, with permanent circulation being ingeniously attached
to one flank of the building. Within the spaces the exhibits, permanent and temporary, can be re-organised at will, providing for many
kinds of different spaces and circulations appropriate to whatever is

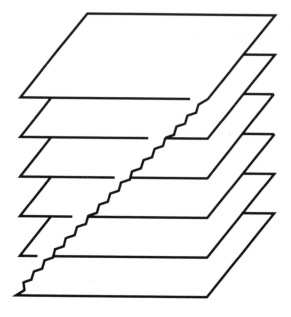

5.2: Simplified diagram of
the Musée Beaubourg Paris.

The Construction of Heritage 90

being shown. This variable topology assumes the variability of categorisations and even the changeable character of knowledges.

These two cases are not, of course, fully comparable, because the first is a permanent collection made originally for purposes of scholarship, and the second is deliberately conceived with elements of showmanship in mind. Moreover, both buildings are exemplars of typical building types that have their own formal traditions and values inscribed into their structure. Nevertheless, the main point will be clear: circulation patterns and spatial hierarchies serve to direct the understanding. The same applies to all exhibitions, permanent or temporary, and to parks.

Interesting cases arise when the curatorial determination to recategorise the collection comes into conflict with the existing architecture. New wings and partitions have to be built, extra doors have to be driven through existing walls. Where this is not possible, a complete re-ordering of the exhibits and their redistribution may be necessary; such an example is provided by the recent 'rehanging' of the Tate Gallery, London, which now tells a different 'history of art' within the same spaces. The Irish Museum of Modern Art at Kilmainham consists of long wide corridors from which smaller rooms open in symmetrical order; this makes it a difficult building in which to stage large inclusive exhibitions. The present director, from both inclination and necessity, has turned this to advantage.

Other conditions arise when an existing building or terrain becomes the object of display – typically, when we are conducted through a great house by a guide, or by following arrows. The route we follow is frequently against the circulation as originally designed. There may, of course, be all manner of good reasons for this, but our experience of the site is mediated by our journey through it and the meanings we derive from it cannot be separated from the particular order in which we encounter its parts. How servants' quarters and the service parts of the house are *met* establishes certain relations; but to experience them spatially one might, for example, require to see the house thrice through different journeys, as 'servant', as 'master', and as 'mistress'. The opportunity for this rarely arises, and so our visits to 'stately homes' are much less revealing than they might be.

In effect, our encounter with objects from the past is mediated by the circumstances in which we meet them – by special buildings, conventions of display, principles of ordering, catalogues, and by the ordering of the spaces in which they are shown; and these are all forms of understanding in their own right.

> Objects do not have an intrinsic meaning which transcends history and context, and a museum is not a neutral space which allows this 'intrinsic' meaning to be displayed. A visit to a museum is a highly mediated experienced in which the 'past' is used as a catalyst –

1. Dodd, L. 'Sleeping with the Past', *CIRCA*, 59 Sept/Oct. 1991, p. 30.

museum displays tell us as much about our attitude to the present as they do about any particular period of the past.[1]

Of all these mediating powers, the narrative provided by architectural space is amongst the most powerful and least regarded by the general public.

I propose to treat this *narrative topology* as a form of rhetoric, which seeks to persuade the visitor. The main distinction I shall make is between directive topologies, which one must follow, and those which are non-directive, and allow individual variations (see below).

My three main headings will be modified, as appropriate, by concepts such as 'coherence and integration' (Topolski), the 'pseudo-event' (Boorstin), 'staged authenticity' (McCannell), and by Cohen's typification of different tourisms. I shall also have recourse to Hadjinicolaou's concept of 'visual ideology' and Hayden White's 'prefiguration' and 'emplotment'.

Though this method has been hatched entirely out of my own brain, something of a like pattern seems to be immanent in the problem of analysis. In the course of my research I came across two shorter studies which follow similar methods: namely Jeffrey Schnapp's investigation of the 1932 'Exhibition of the Fascist Revolution'[2] and a fascinating essay on the 'African Hall' in the American Museum of Natural History, by Donna Haraway.[3]

2. In Schnapp, J.T. 'Epic Demonstrations: Fascist Modernity and the 1932 Exhibition of the Fascist Revolution' in *Fascism, Aesthetics and Culture* R.J. Golsan (ed.) (Hanover and London, Univ. Press of New England 1992).

3. Haraway, D. 'Teddy Bear Patriarchy; Taxidermy in the Garden of Eden; New York 1908–36', *Social Text*, 11, 1984–5, pp. 20–61.

My case studies are chosen for contingent reasons – they were the sites I was most easily able to visit, and for the reason that they all involve permanent structures of some size and seriousness. However, the details of displays alter from time to time, and this should not be read as a guide book. At all times I am chiefly concerned with the general principles of a possible criticism.

I have written and published on two of these examples before, and the question arose as to whether or not to allow my original texts to stand unaltered, or to incorporate them completely into the newer material, thus gaining in intellectual integration what I might be losing in immediacy. I have chosen a middle course, keeping much of the original structure and wording but avoiding repetition or rehearsal of ideas already developed elsewhere. It seems to me important, where a critical strategy is being developed rather than demonstrated conclusively, that one should avoid a premature closure of the terms of argument. There is a tendency for academic method to look for a mechanical kind of certainty, which ought to be resisted. I have, therefore, tried to keep something of the tone and style of my first attempts, and I have not suppressed the desire for conjecture nor the pleasures of polemic. Nor have I burdened these case studies with extensive references.

I begin with an English example for the main reason that the site clearly demonstrates some of my headings – indeed, the terrain was originally designed with some of the concepts in mind; but also because, while not appearing to have controversial implications, it is a good example of what we shall encounter elsewhere.

1. Fountains Abbey and Studley Royal, North Yorkshire

> A visit to Fountains Abbey and Studley Royal is a unique experience. No other site in Europe contains such a variety of monuments from past ages, together giving an unparalleled opportunity to appreciate the range of England's heritage. The wooded valley of the River Skell shelters not only the extensive ruins of Fountains Abbey itself, an outstanding example of the power of medieval monasticism, but also John Aislabie's early 18th century water garden, adorned with classical temples and statues, and the honey-coloured elegance of Fountains Hall, its beautiful late 16th century façade epitomising the confidence of the age. In the deer park beyond the garden lies St Mary's Church, an essay in High Victorian Gothic and the religious masterpiece of the architect William Burges, its florid decoration a striking contrast to the Cistercian simplicity of Fountains. Each of these features is a superb example of its kind. (National Trust Publication 1988)[4]

4. *Fountains Abbey and Studley Royal; North Yorkshire*, National Trust (1988) with text by Mary Mauchline and Lydia Greaves. Informative short essays and excellent photographs.

The National Trust brochure to the park does not mention the first great object that we encounter – the visitor centre designed by Edward Cullinan in 1989–90 and itself a building of note; because it was not then built. This building is a carefully crafted combination of modernist and neo-vernacular elements which is itself worth detailed study.

Narrative Topology

The visitor leaves the centre (which I describe below) by walking through a recently planted wood and across a field. At the time of writing, this wood is still incomplete, but the path, making a serpentine curve through it, is designed to present us with a *coup* – the spectacle of the abbey tower rising abruptly out of the level field, its lower half still hidden in the narrow valley. The path reaches the precipitous edge of the valley and through openings in its wooded fringe affords us carefully managed 'picturesque' views down onto the ruins of the abbey and beyond – the tower still standing high above us.

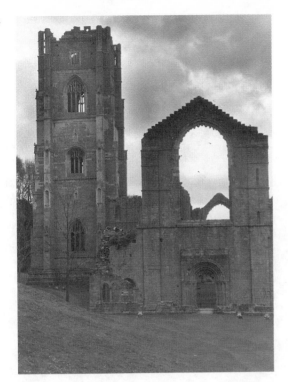

Turning abruptly around we then walk into the ruins of the abbey. Enormous walls of golden limestone, intricate stairways, dark vaults and a roofless nave of cathedral dimensions.

The ensemble is, we realise, enclosed in a narrow thickly wooded declivity, almost a ravine, through which the small river, that once turned millwheels, is guided down carefully engineered channels. From here we can walk down either side of the valley, beside a green lawn for a quarter of a mile until the valley bends abruptly to the left and we enter thick woodland.

5.5

A crescent shaped basin of still water is enclosed in this bend, and the woods open to disclose a temple –

which is succeeded by a rectilinear canal and, as the river bends back right again, by a further canal –

and a semi-circular levelled space containing further ponds and another view across to the temple.

5.8

In the wooded hillsides around are a 'Temple of Fame', an octagonal tower, a 'surprise view' and shelter known as 'Anne Boleyn's seat', and a charming 'Banqueting Hall'.

5.9

There are remnants of other structures. From all the paths, sudden views are afforded of these sights or out over the surrounding countryside through carefully cut openings. These views, and the main axes of the park are aligned upon York Minster, visible many miles away to the south-east, and on Ripon Cathedral closer to hand; thus they construct yet another set of relationships still and draw other great architectural objects into the bounds of the park.

At length we come to a masonry cascade, a parapet, lodges and a lower lake. Here the woodland stops and we are in a broad open deer-park of green grass interspersed with large and very old oak and

 5.10

beech trees. The valley continues, containing several rustic bridges whilst up to our left, on a hillside, is Burges's sturdy little church (not illustrated). The original Studley Royal House was reached from this church by a long avenue, but it was destroyed by fire in 1946; all that remains now is a massive stable block in Palladian style, and an entrance arch (not illustrated).

We return by a variety of ways to the abbey, which is now seen again framed in a surprise view across the lawns, and thence to the centre.

5.11

The journey, particularly in early summer, or on a winter's evening to the accompaniment of rooks, is a delight; but it is a complete reversal of the narrative originally designed into the site by John Aislabie and his son. In its original form one left the house, crossed the land that is now the park (this area was not part of the first design), entered by the lodges and the cascade and walked upstream; the first sight of the abbey was as a picturesque ruin glimpsed through an opening in the trees and then face on at the end of the long lawn. The effect of this reversal is to reduce its range of possible meanings and to muffle the many-layered allegories of political and mercantile power that are, both deliberately and accidentally, inscribed in the complete ensemble, like time through the layers of rocks.

Briefly these 'layers' consist of:

a) Cistercian enterprise. The abbey stood at the centre of a web of roads and trackways linking important mines and mills across a large part of the north of England. The trade in lead and wool, essential to the medieval economy, was extensively organised by Cistercian foundations, whose plain style of building and avoidance of decorative ostentation was a sign of efficiency as much as of piety.

b) Tudor mercantilism. The sale of the abbey buildings by the Crown, and its rapid speculative resale led to the building of Fountains Hall from the stones of the abbey. The design of the building (not illustrated here) rather awkwardly combines medieval and Renaissance elements. Though it has a 'mellow and romantic quality' in the picturesque manner, it is in fact inscribed with a cultural and political revolution of immense significance and brutality.

c) Hanoverian speculation. John Aislabie, who acquired the estate in 1699, created the next strata – the water-garden – as a deliberate and highly self-conscious Anglicisation of a French garden type. The financing of this huge undertaking was inextricably bound up with political adventurism and his 'notorious and most dangerous corruption'. The garden was completed during his long enforced retirement, and in its original form (many details are now obscured) has been interpreted as a political manifesto. The completion of the whole estate and the more picturesque elements in the design were the work of his son William (as was the companion 'sublime' garden at Hackfall nearby, now ruined).

d) Victorian imperialism. St Mary's Church was commissioned from Burges in 1871 by the Marquess of Ripon (Viceroy of India 1880–84). It is an excellent example of nineteenth-century neo-medievalism, being the product of both learned antiquarian study and contemporary method, of the kind discussed in chapter 2 above. It contains the tomb of the patron and his wife lying in marble effigy, simulating the manner of the middle ages.

e) Lastly, the contemporary visitors centre and the re-ordering of the narrative topology embodies the attempt of the National Trust and English Heritage to comprehend all this within the terms of a pleasurable 'unique experience', as part of the ideology of the modern British state.

Visualisation

5. For the concept of 'visual ideology', see Hadjinicolaou, N. *Art History and Class Struggle* (London, Pluto Press 1978). Whilst this book is entirely concerned with art history, it provides a number of useful concepts, in particular 'visual ideology' which is 'the way in which the formal and thematic elements of a picture are combined on each specific occasion. This combination is a particular form of the overall ideology of a social class' (p. 95). This is not simply a translation or transcription of ideas into art, because it has to take into account the highly specific process of the production of pictures as well as an analysis of style in relation to class. It is 'a theoretical concept which allows us a better grasp of the particularities of the production of pictures and its history. This history is none other than the history of visual ideologies' (p. 98). It is clear that this concept, used with care, may be applied to wider fields, including the design of gardens and parks.

6. See Hussey, C. *English Landscapes and Gardens 1700–1750* (London, Country Life Ltd 1967).

7. In what follows I am indebted to Patrick Eyres, and to his essay, 'Studley Royal and Hackfall; The Classical and Sublime landscapes of North Yorkshire', *New Arcadians' Journal*, 20, Winter 1985. And more generally to the activities of Ian Hamilton Finlay and his commentators such as Stephen Bann.

8. The Speaker of the House of Commons, *cf.* Hussey, ibid.

9. Eyres, op. cit., p. 10.

Recent studies of English landscape design have shown, quite clearly, how gardens and parks were used as exemplars of taste, and how that taste was perceived in national–political terms as a 'visual ideology'.[5] Statues, follies, temples and towers were used to focus and make explicit emblematic environments.[6] In the case of Studley Royal, there are self-justificatory and polemical intentions to be read from original design and its developments.[7]

John Aislabie was an adroit and unscrupulous politician, siding now with Whigs and now with Tories in the shifting administrations of the early eighteenth century. His attitude to the public purse was shared by most politicians of the day and is remarkable mainly by reason of its *extreme* rapacity. 'He was a man of good understanding, no ill speaker in Parliament, but dark and of a cunning that rendered him suspected. He was much set on increasing his fortune . . .'[8] His attempt to 'privatise' the national debt, known as the South Sea Bubble, collapsed in extraordinary scenes in 1720. Impeached and virtually banished, Aislabie retreated to Yorkshire with his remaining considerable wealth. Patrick Eyres, who has paid close attention to what is known of the original designs and has correlated them with Aislabie's political fortunes and allegiances, has interpreted Studley Royal gardens as an allegory based upon the polarities of 'prudence' and 'passion', upon the contrast between the private and the public realms, in which erotic symbolism and allusions played a large part. 'Far from being a country retreat, the . . . garden manifests a committed political and cultural counter-attack on affairs in the exterior world.'[9]

A similar polemical intention inspired the gardens at Stowe and Chiswick, created by Lords Cobham and Burlington respectively after their loss of office. Aislabie's approach to landscape was shared by literary 'Hanoverian Tories' such as Swift, Steele and Pope, and by architects such as Vanburgh and Campbell.

Aislabie *fils* continued this tradition by creating features that memorialised the capture of Quebec, the conquest of Canada, and the victories at sea. His purchase of Fountains Abbey and Hall enabled him to complete the present park with the culminating 'picturesque' device of the framed view of ruins and the long approach. The original effect was, we may assume, something in the nature of a journey back through time toward the picturesque origins of the present. Seen in a more materialist light, the purchase of the abbey and hall brought a long feud to an end – the family from whom the abbey was purchased was the remaining wealthy Catholic family of the area. The aestheticisation of the past was accompanied by drawing a line under its capacity to affect the future.

The park was, therefore, a social and political statement of some complexity. Its mode of *visualisation* however has been eroded by time and the meaning of the statues and buildings and special sites have been lost, altered, and overlaid. In particular, the precisely alleg-orical aspects of the design have been overlaid by the picturesque; firstly, those picturesque elements stressed by William Aislabie (which seem to have softened the more aggressive neo-classicism of his father), and then by those which the National Trust has itself imposed – what we might call the 'neo-picturesque' – by way of its new footpaths and viewing stations. The neo-picturesque creates a frame through which to view the original, tending further to 'har-monise' the original significance. To walk through the grounds is to traverse a palimpsest whose meanings have to be uncovered in layers.

By reversing the *narrative topology* the whole terrain, considered from the picturesque point of view, has been turned inside out. There is no clear focus for the 'unique experience'. We are invited to view the abbey in the picturesque mode, but back to front; this puts a double screen of aestheticisation between us and the abbey as an historical 'document' – that screen created by the Aislabies's original concept, and then that provided by the Trust's narration. The Trust, in its accompanying literature, though informative about the history, does not make this clear, and though it alludes to the shifts in power that created the terrain, it provides no adequate explanation of what this means *on the ground* and *to the eye*.

Simulation

The idea of *simulation* does not at first appear appropriate to this example, except in so far as the Aislabie garden (in both its layers) is itself a kind of simulation of literary and pictorial models. But closer enquiry reveals that the original designs were part of a series of simulations, or representations of representations going back to classical times but mediated or moderated by contemporary con-cerns. In a similar way, Burges's church simulates its real medieval prototypes further up the valley, as the patron's tomb simulates those of the knight and his lady.

Without that scholarship – which is of a kind not easily accessible to most visitors – we are presented with a rich and beautiful place to whose historical meanings we have very largely lost the key. Thus our experience of it – which is part of the creation of its modern meaning – is frustrated. Its history, in fact, has been generalised into an atmos-phere that is potent, but vague. The pleasurable and picturesque aspects of the park have been accentuated at the expense of the emblematic ideology of the garden. In Cohen's terms, 'recreational' and 'diversionary' tourism wins out over the 'experiential' mode. In

White's terms, the history of the site has been 'pre-figured' to provide for an uncontroversial historical reading, in which irreconcilable oppositions have been harmonised. We have to conclude that, as a form of popular history, the Studley Royal/Fountains Abbey complex, though providing a pleasant experience, is unsatisfying.

Investigating the original significance of the park is a form of archaeology; to demonstrate the findings to visitors would require some kind of interpretive intervention. Who can deliver us some of those historical coherences, that intellectual integration, in which historical truth consists? It is here that the nature and purpose of the visitor centre and the associated literature become important.

5.12: Neo-vernacular meets neo-modern; the visitors centre at Studley Royal (arch. E. Cullinan 1992).

This building was designed by Edward Cullinan and his office in 1992 and in plan consists of an open square enclosed by two L-shaped pavilions.[10] These pavilions are roofed with local slates and lead, and faced with local stone (like the Yorkshire barns which they resemble from a distance), and with cinnamon-coloured cedar planks which are now beginning to weather with a silvery sheen. The essential structure of the building, however, is of white-painted steel. It is, therefore, a design that is deliberately bi-natured. On the one hand, in open plan and technology it is 'neo-modernist', and on the other, in external materials and distant elevation it is 'neo-vernacular'. (This is a characteristic Cullinan combination; his office has a fine reputation for fitting thoroughly modern buildings into historically sensitive sites, using such means appropriately adapted.)

This double nature comes together in some of the detailing. The steel posts and beams meet and link together with ingenious and carefully crafted brackets; the dry stone walls (which simulate the typical field divisions of the region) act as rain screens; the cedar boards are fixed with exposed wooden dowels.

Colin Davies in *The Architectural Review* writes: 'This habit of displaying all the constructional nuts and bolts gives the building a satisfying, solidly crafted quality. . . . It is a lesson in building construction that a child of five could understand.'[11] The interiors are a delight; the high curving ceilings are faced with birch ply-wood, and the cedar planks let light through in glimmering shafts. The services and toilets are of the very highest quality.

There is an historical exhibition which adds nothing to the existing literature, and a book and gift shop. These serve to confirm the experience of the re-arranged narrative and to set it in an ambience of diversion and easy charm. It is to the building itself we must look for the inner character of the whole experience. There is no doubt that this is a building of distinction, which lives up to the site it is called on to introduce; but from the perspective of our critical method, what does it tell us about 'heritage'?

The clients (the National Trust and English Heritage), working with the architect, are making a statement. They have quoted William Morris to align themselves with the past as 'continuers of history'.[12] The completed centre combines new materials with old, and while its plan is 'modern', its elevation is 'picturesque'. It is not so very far from the idea of a 'national character' (that is actually 'English' rather than 'British'), and from Webb's 'Red House' of 1858, despite the obvious differences of style. We are clearly dealing with another and contemporary example of visual ideology at work; one which asserts one of the ideological pillars of the British state during the past hundred and fifty years – the principle of continuity through change, and the refusal

10. A useful critical description will be found in *The Architectural Review*, Nov. 1992.

11. Ibid.

12. See Davies, ibid. I have not been able to trace the publication that he cites.

of 'catastrophic' explanations. It is doing the same kind of work as we have seen performed by Walter Scott's novels: 'accounting for social change, and explaining even comparatively recent changes to a world that [is] beginning to lose touch with its past'.[13] Thus the Visitor Centre is itself a deeply ideological structure; its visual language is closely allied to the rhetoric of a conservative state.

But a closer reading of the site that the building introduces reveals a very different reality, because Fountains Abbey and Studley Royal embody a history of sudden interventions and appropriations – of the dissolution of the monasteries in order to make way for the secular state, of a cultural revolution, the rise of a new class, of corruption on the grandest scale, of the aestheticisation of power and the simulation of the past; the rhetoric of its narrative persuades us of the 'natural' course of these events, without any sense of their aggressive character. What there is of continuity in this story is likely to be an *ex post facto* reconstruction to serve some particular interest.

Thus the reversed narrative and the 'neo-picturesque' insertions into the Aislabie's design, and the assertion of the 'recreational' and 'diversionary' values, serve an end – which is to make history more pleasant and less problematic. The Visitor Centre, as both the start and the finish of the narrative, sums up the unspoken intent.

13. See ch. 2, note 5 etc.

5.13 Construction detail

An unspoken intent in one circumstance may be dismissed as harmless (though if we are concerned with historical truth we shall be sceptical); in other circumstances, the unspoken may indeed speak loudly. It is with this in mind that we turn to our next example. . . .

2. The Ulster–American Folk Park, Omagh[14]

14. Earlier versions of this section have appeared in *CIRCA*, 53 Sept/Oct. 1990, and in O'Connor and Cronin (eds.) (1993).

> Sail away to the New World on the brig *Union* and meet us at work in our kitchens and farms.
>
> Stroll around the grounds of the Ulster–American Folk Park and enjoy a few hours of living history. Visit the authentically-furnished thatched cottages of Rural Ulster and the log cabins of frontier America and you will be sure of a warm welcome from our costumed interpreters as they busy themelves at their everyday tasks. Turf fires, the aroma of baked bread and the clicking of the spinning wheel all contributed to the special atmosphere of bygone days. You will learn a great deal about the lives of the thousands of men, women and children who left in the eighteenth and nineteenth centuries to seek their fortunes in the New World of America.
>
> You can even travel with them on board the emigrant ship and experience the sounds, smells and dreadful conditions of life at sea.
> (Brochure: the Ulster–American Folk Park 1992)

The park is situated in a broad and beautiful valley some miles north of Omagh. Here, several acres of rough ground have been laid out with a walk which emerges from a visitors centre (which includes a static exhibition on emigration to America and a series of tableaux) and leads in a numbered sequence around a series of Ulster cottages and other reassembled buildings, including a Presbyterian church, before taking us by way of a street, a port and quayside (housed in a large building), through the hold of a ship (complete with sound effects, smells and fellow passengers) into an 'America' complete with maple trees, cleared fields and carpentered wooden houses. On the way we meet inhabitants engaged in household tasks, offering oatcakes and scones made according to old recipes and telling us harrowing tales of their voyage. Nearby is a building holding a small but very useful library relating to emigration.

The exhibits are all interesting and some are moving. The church/meeting house presents us with an image of ecclesiastical democracy in action: austere, orderly and egalitarian beyond anything existing today. There is an attention to detail throughout which is admirable and also unpretentious. There is sometimes a sharp sense of having surprised another form of society in an unguarded moment, which goes some way toward persuading us that this is indeed an 'authentic' experience. There is no doubt that this park is greatly enjoyed by visitors.

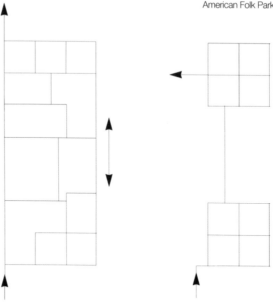

Simplified plan of directive and non-directive circulation in Northern Ireland Folk Park, Cultra

Simplified plan of directive and non-directive dirculation in the Ulster–American Folk Park, Omagh

The *topology* contains, however, an element of compulsion; to see it in full we must follow the correct procedure. In this it is different from its sister organisation, the Northern Ireland Folk Park at Cultra, Co. Down. A comparison of their respective circulation plans reveals this quite clearly. In the first case, though there is a natural flow to the progress of the paths between exhibits, and signs encourage one route rather than another, it is quite possible to wander in other directions, or to reverse direction. There is no one necessary order, and so no single narrative. At Omagh, however, the visitors must pass through the strait-gate of the emigrant ship. They move from an 'Ulster' – stone built, whitewashed, thatched and densely wooded – into an 'America' that is cleared and planted with rectilinear and carpentered houses. Though in either sector we can move freely about, there is only one way from one sector to the other, and that (like emigration?) is irreversible.

In this respect, the circulation pattern at Omagh embodies the experience of the Mellon family whose gift of land and finance initiated the project, and with them, the experience of many thousands of others who emigrated and can only return under another heading – that of the tourist.

The crucial passage (the word is chosen for all its senses) is the progress from the quayside, on board ship and through the holds where we encounter tableaux of suffering and hear tales of misery. The subsequent emergence into the light of the 'American' countryside from the enclosed, almost subterranean, world of the ship is a considerable *coup de théâtre* whose place in the narrative structure is that which, in an initiation ceremony, would be represented by the removal of a blindfold. We have been reborn into another level of existence. The narrative form is that of an initiation. The role played by the eating of 'authentic' oatcakes in the first habitation we encounter is exactly that of a ritual meal; it confirms membership of the new society and establishes a new order of reality.

(We should note in passing that the use of smell and taste on these occasions is important because of the highly evocative and 'primitive' character of these senses. In the sensual hierarchy of Euro-American culture, taste and smell stand for the 'nature' that is to be controlled and ordered by sight. An intrusion of smells, in particular, is an intrusion of the uncontrollable. It appears in heritage simulations as an attempot to establish the 'natural' (i.e. successfully simulated) character of the display. Taste, too, fixes the place in memory so that it comes to be remembered as a real rather than simulated experience. The gritty texture and harsh taste of an oatcake remains the most vivid recollection I have of 'America'.)

Our progress through the park can most easily be shown by a 'story-board', namely:

5.15

We go to a thatched forge . . .

5.16 . . . to a cottage in the woods . . .

5.17 . . . to the meeting house . . .

5.18 . . . down a shady lane . . .

5.19 . . . into the street . . .

5.20 . . . and pass by an arch . . .

5.21 . . . into the hold of a ship . . .

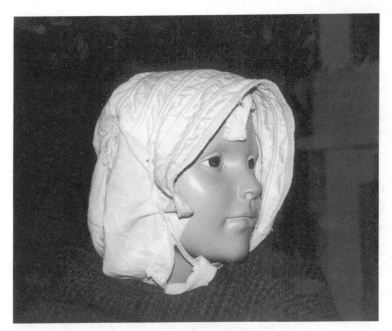

5.22 . . . meeting strange faces . . .

5.23 . . . thence by a narrow place . . .

5.24 . . . into a cleared land . . .

5.25 . . . of neat houses . . .

5.26 . . . and rectilinear gardens . . .

5.27 . . . in 'Pennsylvania'.

The initiation is an archetypal narrative structure, whose function is to reveal hidden truths; it is this ritual aspect that prevents the park from delivering the explanatory investigation and integration which is what we expect from 'history'. I propose that what we are offered is a *mythical structure*. As Roland Barthes has observed, 'Myth gets rid of something. It does away with the complexity of human actions and bestows upon them the simplicity of essences.'[15]

15. Barthes, R.
Mythologies (Paris,
Editions Seuil),
p. 231.

This mythical structure is revealed through a study of the system of binary opposites through which 'Ulster' and 'America' are defined and through the process of designing the park, *visualised* and subsequently *simulated*: thus . . .

Ulster	America
stone	wood
thatch	shingle
shaggy	smooth
grazed	planted
dense	cleared
'natural'	'rational'
'picturesque'	'modern'

The two parts of the park are presented as the difference to each other's norm.

Such a system of oppositions bears a most uncertain relation to the reality of settlement in the New World. The seventeenth and eighteenth-century immigrants were travelling to a land a good deal more 'shaggy', 'dense' and 'natural' than the place they were leaving. This binary system is a retrospective construction of the difference between the two realms (hence, in Topolski's terms, a manifestation of the time-consciousness that we find in *chronicles* rather than in *scholarly history*), and in another sense (at another strata) a reflection of the early Presbyterian concept of Ireland as a 'new-found land' to be cleared and planted and made rational. In the creation of the park, 'Ulster' has been imagined as the 'Ireland' that still exists in the mind of many Northerners and most British.

The opposition that is inscribed in the topology and visual imagery of the park is extremely ancient. It dates from the very earliest foreign accounts of Ireland, which themselves contained and perpetuated a comparative strategy that set the civilised against the barbarous. In the twelfth century, Giraldus Cambrensis, in his *History and Topography of Ireland* prepared the way for the park by defining the 'Irish' as *gens sylvestris*, forest-dwellers:

> This is a people of forest-dwellers, and inhospitable; a people living off beasts and like beasts; a people that still adheres to the most primitive way of pastoral living. For as humanity progresses from the forests to

arable fields, and towards village life and civil society, this people is too lazy for agriculture and is heedless of material comfort; and they positively dislike the rules and legalities of civil intercourse; thus they have been unable and unwilling to abandon their traditional life of forest and pasture.[16]

To make the whole matter more complicated, there is a good argument to be made (following Chapman, 1992) that this simulation of 'Ireland' is merely the latest term in a series of oppositions between civil and barbarous people that began when ancient Greeks first designated the peoples to their north as *keltoi*; a nomenclature which was continued well into the Middle Ages by the Byzantine geographers and which owes far more to a demand for spatial symmetry than to real geography.[17] Such an argument tends to collapse the very notion of 'Celtic Ireland' into an infinite series of moves in a discourse – a 'precession' of immense depth.

By escaping from forest life (emigrating to America), we become civilised ('rational'). Thus, the park argues, the 'Ulster' that we left is the 'Ireland' that we arrived in to subdue; and the 'America' we arrived in is the 'Ulster' we created out of 'Ireland'. (Just how this is understood by American visitors I have no way of knowing. I think we must assume that for the children of emigrants, this park is an 'existential' visit;[18] whereas for the more casual visitor, diversion is the main good.)

By this interpretation, the park is an enactment of the deep logical structure of the process from pastoralism to the Enlightenment and modernity, whereby the wilderness has to be repudiated and a higher level of discipline achieved. But an enactment is a ritual form, whose premises are symbolic and largely unconscious – and therefore ahistorical. In the course of this ritual, rational interpretation has to be abandoned and 'immediate' confrontation (actually a 'staged authenticity' according to McCandless) preferred. *Simulation* is the essential device.

The enactment is vividly experienced by the way in which the re-assembled buildings of 'America' – actually, Pennsylvania – are experienced. As the visitor emerges from the hold of the ship, and up the narrow ramp (which hides the sight of 'America' until the very last moment), he or she is confronted with some beautiful and simple wooden houses. These are utterly unlike those in 'Ulster'. Adzed and sawn slabs of timber (certainly not 'logs') are jointed into one another and faced with neat shingles of grooved planks. The spaces between them are smoothed out with white-painted plaster. The aesthetic is tense, geometric, undecorated and highly organised around a rectilinear grid. Nothing that we have seen has prepared us for this, except perhaps the timbers of the Meeting House roof. There is a rhetoric, but it is the puritan rhetoric of the 'plain and perspicacious style'.[19]

16. *The History and Topography of Ireland* ed. and trans. J.J. O'Meara. (Harmondsworth, Penguin 1982), book 3, ch. 10. Since discovering this passage I find it has also been cited in a paper by Joep Leerssen. 'Wildness, Wilderness, and Ireland: Medieval and Early-modern Patterns in the Demarcation of Civility', *Journal of the History of Ideas*, 56, 1, January 1995, pp. 25–39.

17. See Chapman, op. cit., ch. 3, p. 129, and esp. ch. 1.

18. See Cohen, op. cit., p. 191: 'We spoke of the "existential" tourist as one who adheres to an 'elective centre'. Such a centre may be completely extraneous to his culture of origin, the history of his society or his biography. But it may also be a traditional centre to which he, his forebears or his "people" had been attached in the past, but become alienated from. In this case, the desire for a visit to such a centre derives from a desire to find one's spiritual roots. The visit takes on the quality of a home-coming to an historical home . . .'

19. 'Truth is indeed clear and simple; it has small need of the argument of the tongue or of eloquence. If it is perspicacious and plain, it has enough support in itself . . .' John Jewel *Oratio contra Rhetoricam* (1548). 'Plainnesse and perspicuity, both for matter and manner of expression are the whole thing . . .', Arch. W. Hooker *Church Discipline* (1648).

These houses present us with a genuine historical problem. There is very little precedent for this method of timber construction in British or Irish vernacular architecture, which typically used timber for a frame which was then filled with brick or lath-and-plaster walling, or faced with boards. The houses in 'America', however, are massive carpentry of a highly individual kind. There are affinities with Alpine and Scandinavian housing and perhaps some Dutch building, in the manner of timber construction, but hardly any of style. Are we looking at housing types devised by shipwrights? Were the first builders Anglo-Dutch ships' carpenters? Looked at from a technological point of view, these houses presuppose a timber industry of some scale, with saw-pits, possibly mechanised, and readily available good quality tools. Are these houses the outcome of the Irish timber trade? We recall that the Ulster plantations were as much the outcome of an insatiable demand for timber, as for any other demand, since Ulster represented the last large-scale resource of oak woods in the islands. Or, more likely, are we looking at a translation of the frame-and-board houses of the North Sea coast into a distinctly American idiom under the stimulus of limitless raw material and a technological and puritan spirit? To penetrate this problem is to get into the heart of a long and difficult set of questions about the relations between culture, technology and the natural environment.

We do not expect the park to resolve these points, but, because the sudden confrontation with this architecture occurs at the climax of the narrative, we ought (if we are doing history) to show that this is an issue. Otherwise the new architecture is a mysterious 'given'.

To make the problem more complex still, it is probably the case that the early settlers were inscribing their Utopian ambitions into their domestic building, and that the geometrical simplicity of their barns and houses connoted the four-square Heavenly City and the Temple itself whose earthly archetype was Solomon's Temple:

> And he built the walls of the house within with boards of cedar, both the floor of the house and the walls of the ceiling; and covered them on the inside with wood, and covered the floor of the house with planks of fir. (1, *Kings* 6:15)[20]

20. Nor is it accidental that these visual/plastic attributes were incorporated into the building technology of Chicago and into the canon of architectural 'modernism'.

This gives the whole narrative an additional layer of meaning: the commitment, the voyage, and the landing become not only figures for initiation and rebirth, but also for the pilgrim's progress 'from this world to that which is to come . . . wherein is discovered the manner of his setting out, his dangerous journey and safe arrival at the desired country'. Bunyan's account of his pilgrim's progress was frequently printed with an imaginary 'road-map' which led the reader out through the Wicket Gate, to Vanity Fair and Doubting Castle and hence to the Celestial City. Such maps resemble the maps of 'theme parks'.

As we have seen, such resemblance is not fortuitous, since all parks have themes; and theme parks are related to the eighteenth-century philosophical and polemical gardens and landscapes we have already studied. Prescribed walks or carriage drives enabled concepts of public life and privacy, of power, of nature and culture to be seen allegorically. The Ulster–American Folk Park, seen in this way, becomes a philosophical garden for a 'Protestant tradition', figured and emplotted according to the symbolism of the *Progress*, and in its mythical aspects an enactment of spiritual rebirth.

The purpose of a mythical structure, according to Mircea Eliade, is to reject 'profane, continuous time' and thereby give human actions a metaphysical 'valorization'.

> But this valorization is emphatically not that which certain post-Hegelian philosophical currents – notably Marxism, historicism and existentialism – have sought to give it since the discovery of 'historical man', of the man who is insofar as he makes himself, within history.[21]

Within such a mythic structure, individuals only become *real* through their participation in and re-enactment of the exemplary model – in this case, the *Pilgrim's Progress*. In the original settlement of America an 'act of creation' was being enacted – 'the transformation of chaos into cosmos'.[22] Far from being an 'immediate' encounter with 'living history' the park embodies and manipulates a network of associations based upon a profound archetype.

The degree to which this manipulation is fully intentional is not easy to ascertain. Detailed documents relating to the inception and development of the park are not available, and it is my guess that they would reveal little. I hypothesise that the narrative structure grew out of a single 'good idea' that was then developed on the one hand by historical scholarship, and on the other for the purposes of recreational tourism, without the two ever being brought together for critical analysis. Nor is it easy to see just what sort of critical analysis could have been employed at the time, there being no 'theory of heritage' available. What has happened – as quite often in the world of popular entertainment and popular history – is that in the ruck of bringing off a considerable feat, the unconscious imagery, its figurative grounding, has remained unconscious. In this respect the park illustrates Eliade's general theory that 'popular memory restores to the historical personage of modern times its meaning as imitator of the archetype and reproducer of archetypal gestures'.[23] I shall return to a fuller discussion of mythical structures in relation to popular history in my conclusion.

21. Eliade, M. 'The Myth of the Eternal Return or, Cosmos and History', trans. W. Trask (New Jersey, Princeton UP, Bollingen series XLVI, 1954), p. ix.

22. Ibid., p. 10.

23. Ibid., p. 44.

Nor, of course, are the visitors manipulated without their willed complicity. McCandless's concept of 'staged authenticity' is a very useful servant, but a bad master. In writing of the 'inauthenticity' of modern life (which he does on many pages) he neglects the humorous irony with which tourists approach their goals. Though we may be moved to a sense of historical piety toward our ancestors, this is strictly within the limits of empathy and play. As Cohen points out (very appositely, in this case)

> The aesthesis provoked by direct contact with the authenticity of others may reassure and uplift the tourist, but does not provide a new meaning and guidance to his life. This can best be seen where 'experiential' tourists observe pilgrims at a pilgrimage centre; the pilgrims experience the sacredness of the centre; the tourist may experience aesthetically the authenticity of the pilgrim's experience.[24]

24. See Cohen, op. cit., p. 188.

What has not remained unconscious, but is certainly not stated directly, is that the premises on which the park is organised are sectarian. That the family home of an important Catholic figure has recently been included does not alter this. The park is not neutrally Ulster–American in a geographic sense, but Ulster–Presbyterian–American in a confessional sense. As it stands at present, it is possible to pass through the experience of the park without ever being made aware of this. The history with which it deals is pre-eminently that of the voluntaristic movements inspired in large part by religious and political idealism. There is small sense of the wretchedness that made the mass emigrations of the nineteenth century a matter of human survival and which were, of course, extensively Catholic and driven by economic necessity. This is a partial, and to say the least, an uncritical view of Ulster.[25]

25. When an earlier version of this essay was published in 1993, a 'loyalist' periodical described me as a member of a 'Dublin-based, Euro-financed and American inspired coterie' who would 'receive corrective therapy, when the facts were known'.

There is, I think, no objection to a sectarian view of history, and none at all to the celebration of the importance of Ulster Protestants in the creation of the United States. The intellectual lineage of Dissent leads directly toward the Constitution, and it is a lineage with which this writer can happily identify. But there are serious objections to not stating one's premises openly. What has happened in this instance is that the partiality has been inscribed in the very form of the experience, in its topology. *Thus it cannot be disentangled from the content.*

I began this study by asserting the importance of popular history. 'In so far as heritage attempts to present a popular history . . . it must be taken seriously.' The difficulty that the park presents to us, is one which is undergone by any attempt in this difficult area – to set a bound to the powers of myth.

It is with these reflections in mind that I now turn to the third of these case-studies.

3. Interpreting the Interpreter: the Navan Fort Centre, Armagh[26]

Navan Fort is a large and ancient earthwork on a hill outside Armagh. Under its ancient name of Emain Macha it is reputed to have been the seat of the kings of Ulster, and it appears in legendary histories. The centre, which is listed in the *Yellow Pages* as a tourist attraction rather than a museum or cultural centre, introduces the visitor to Navan Fort to a combination of artefacts (real and simulated), tableaux and audio-visual displays of several kinds; all housed in a striking and attractive building. This building, technically speaking a berm, is largely hidden under a mound of earth which alludes to the fort itself.[27]

We can note in passing that the design of 'visitor' and 'interpretive' buildings has become an architectural genre in its own right, in which the aim is to produce as fine a structure as possible without seeming so to do. The symbolism of some of these buildings deserves study, because they seek to naturalise their own existence and to disappear into the site. The 'friendliness' may be part of a strategy whereby the difficulties, contradictions and ugliness of history are accommodated to contemporary taste. In the case of Navan, the centre somewhat resembles the restored burial mound of Newgrange, except that it is unobtrusively located in a hollow, and has doors, skylights and an attractive terrace.

a) Topology

The plan of the building or site is, of course, the essential and guiding element in the whole; in this case, the topology of the visitor's experience is determined and uni-directional. Once entered, circulation cannot be reversed without embarrassment. I will begin with a simple description of this journey; my aim is not yet to criticise, but to understand just what kind of an experience is offered.

We enter down a pathway which leads to a narrowing courtyard set into the side of the mound. The sides are of well-crafted, irregular mortarless stone and they curve inward to a substantial porch with large wooden pillars; a glass door with 'Celtic' motif slides open automatically, leading to a vestibule which, still narrowing, leads to a substantial wooden door, which opens with a satisfying noise to let you into a circular atrium, with more wooden pillars and a domed skylight. Here there is an information desk, a small shop with a mixture of souvenirs and more scholarly reading, and a pleasant self-service café opening onto the terrace. Around the atrium, between the pillars and above head height are large images of the warriors, horses and maidens who we meet again, beyond.

There is also space for exhibitions of paintings and photographs; on my first visit there were some striking photographs by Chris

26. This section has been published in *CIRCA* and given as a paper at the Douglas Hyde Conference 1994 in Ballaghaderreen Co. Roscommon. I am using an emended version of that paper here.

27. An easily available account of the building will be found in *Perspective; Journal of the RSUA* Sept./Oct. 1993. The building was designed by McAdam Design (John Crothers; partner in charge) and the exhibition devised by Ideas Ltd., Interpretative Consultants, of York (project designer, Stephen Howe; graphic designer Helen Louise Wood). The audio-visual aspects were realised by Centre Screen Productions of Manchester. I am assuming that Centre Screen Productions were commissioned by Ideas Ltd. It is not clear who was responsible for the script and the original art-work. The ultimate responsibility for the format of the whole exhibition must rest with whatever committee wrote the original brief. My interest, of course, is with the general principles guiding heritage and visitor centres as such. Everyone connected with the project was very helpful to me, and it is rather mortifying to lay into the centre in this manner. My argument, however, is that these naïveties and contradictions inhere in the very concept of 'heritage' and 'interpretation' and the demand of the tourist industry for unproblematic representations.

28. C.D. Friedrich (1774–1842), German painter of notably 'sublime' landscapes.

Hill and Jill Jennings on display, which portrayed the site and other ancient locations in a light drawn from the paintings of Caspar David Friedrich.[28]

The 'show' itself is in three parts: 'The Dawning', 'The Real World' and 'The Other World'. 'The Dawning' consists of a small lobby and a mixed display of tableaux and video images; its theme is the real history of the site, since glacial times, and its legendary history as the source of stories. There are representations and film of story-telling and of the simultaneous arrival of writing and Christianity, and a disquisition on the European background of the Celts – 'part of our common European heritage'. When this is completed, a door opens and you are invited through into the next stage.

In 'The Real World' we encounter the findings of archaeology, with real and simulated artefacts, explanatory placards, interactive video screens and sound effects. This space is divided into different areas by tree-trunk screens, and the light levels are low. I have described the topology as uni-directional and determined, but at this point the 'real world' is open to exploration; we can wander around in it from one zone to another at our own will. The interactive

5.28 The Navan Fort Centre – simulating its own topic.

5.29

5.30

5.31

5.32

5.33

5.34

videos afford virtual 'windows' that look into other spaces and other sites, with controllable options and by-ways. This visitor, at least, learnt of things he did not know before, and enjoyed doing so. If you press a button, you hear the sound of one of the Loughnashade horns, and a very powerful and eerie sound it is, like a didgeridoo sostenuto. Experientially as well as spatially, the 'real world' offers alternatives, and raises questions. Navan Fort is offered as a problem of interpretation.

After about thirty minutes another door opens and we encounter a theatre, 'The Other World', with the effect of dappled water-reflected light, music, and a screen area on which, over some forty minutes, we watch condensed and lively versions of the stories of Deirdre and Cúchulain. This is presented to us through the device of a monk who tells us he is setting down these stories ('which may not be true, but ought to be') in between writing down the gospels. There is an ingenious mix of video, laser holography, film animation and light-show, for which no less than nine different projectors are required, all done with bravura and some sensibility. A sound-track makes a great use of keening voices and synthesised drumming. When this is concluded the lights come up, a door opens, and we are returned to the atrium, from whence we are free to walk pleasantly up to the real Fort of Navan, and reflect on what we have seen.

This sequence has been sharply criticised, especially in Northern Ireland, from two main (and interlinked) points of view. In the first place, the mingling of the real and the simulated, the archaeological and the poetical, is merely promiscuous, not revelatory. In the second, the retelling of the Cúchulain story and its refrain is only too easily given a political interpretation. That refrain, repeated several times in the telling goes – 'This is a bad day for Ulster. And a worse day for you.' (Readers who do not know the 'Táin' need to understand here that the story recounts the attempted invasion of Ulster by Queen Maeve and the armies of Ireland, and the heroic single-handed defence of the border by the magical hero Cúchulain, the 'Hound of Ulster'.) On the day of my first visit yet another murder was inflicted on Armagh. In the week during which I sat down to write this page I went to the funeral of a man who had lost his life in active service. I am not sure how far it is understood on the southern side of the border that the Cúchulain story has been thoroughly appropriated by extreme 'loyalism'; but the tendentiousness of the story is obvious enough.[29] I know of people who have felt compelled to walk out of the exhibition on these grounds.

At the same time, critics and academic writers have to acknowledge that the centre is popular, that children get great delight from the experience, and that the archaeology is real and enlightening. The

29. For a discussion of this phenomenon, and the writings of Ian Adamson and others, see *Fortnight* magazine, 320: 'More Annals of Ulster' by W.A. Hanna, and 321: 'Deceptions of Demons' by H.J. Morgan. A large mural has recently appeared in Lower Newtownards Road, Belfast, depicting Cúchulain as 'defender of Ulster against Ireland'. This image of the hero is derived from Oliver Shepherd's statue. For further uses of this image, see an article by John Turpin in *CIRCA*, 69, 'Cúchulainn Lives On', (pp. 26–31).

question for the moment, however, is not criticism but analytic description; what is the nature of the experience the centre offers us?

Looked at phenomenologically, the topology returns us to the body; at first to the womb, later, perhaps the digestive tract. The image that came to this visitor was of the cow's three stomachs. The journey through the three realms is spatially disorienting and we are expelled (regurgitated?) back into the atrium when we expected to find ourselves in the open air. The plan of the centre is, in fact, based geometrically on two interlocked circles; a figure which produces a rich configuration of arcs and angles and unusual lobbies but because we don't know this unless we look at the diagram of the emergency exits, our spatial 'reading' of the place is constantly challenged. Because the elevation of the building is largely hidden by earth banks and greenery, it cannot be 'read' from outside, either. The further you go in, the bigger it seems. This is like the story of the young man who . . . There are whole sets of metaphors inscribed and active in this narrative structure and topology. In sum, the building as Sheila-na-gig.[30]

b) Simulation

Simulation is an essential, not merely ancillary, feature of the centre, and it begins with the building which simulates the fort it interprets, and interprets by simulation. The mound, the greenery, the passage, the timber structure within are more than allusions; they repeat or rhyme with the original structure. At the mythical level, it simulates the hollow hill that contains the 'other world' of vanished and supernatural heroism.

Simulation, too, has a major role in the three-stage exhibition; not always successfully.[31] 'The Dawning' contains a revolving tableau with dummy figures, which does not blend happily with the much slicker imagery on the screen. 'The Real World' is far from uniformly real, since it contains real objects mixed with simulations in fibreglass, and it is not quite clear, or easily overlooked, which are the real and which are the 'false'. It is necessary to put the word false in between quotes here, because this realm is already a mixed domain. If there is an objection, it is not to simulation, but to the fact of that simulation not being self-evident. Simulation too plays a part in 'The Other World', over and above the imaginary aspect; the show is introduced and closed by the presence of two large Celtic 'carvings' appearing at us out of the dark.

The crucial issue in any discussion of simulation is not the simulacrum, but the status of the real. 'Too strong an insistence on a particular understanding of "reality" and "authenticity" may only serve to conceal other inauthenticities, or suppress other possible

30. My idea of architectural phenomenology derives largely from Gaston Bachelard (*The Poetics of Space* (1964)) and the writings of Christian Norberg Schulze, esp. *Existence Space and Architecture* (London, Thames and Hudson 1971).

31. The use of dummies in exhibitions and historical sites is commented on by Charles Brett in *Ulster Architect*, 3: 4, March 1994: 'I would urge that all those concerned with the propagation of stuffed dummies in architectural contexts to exercise the utmost self-restraint.'

realities.'[32] Our critique of the simulacrum must be balanced by a corresponding critique of the concept of the real that is being simulated; or else we lose ourselves in a dualistic dilemma of the authentic versus the false. Or what is worse, fall into what Baudrillard has described as the 'precession of simulacra' in which one follows another with no 'real' at the start or end to which thay can be referred.[33]

It is one thing to have a simulated carving next to real artefacts in an informational situation as in 'The Real World'; another thing to have a simulated carving used to introduce an imaginative fantasia on epic themes, in a fictional 'Other World'. But in using the very phrase 'informational situation' I am falling into my own trap, because the notion that real artefacts are, in themselves, clearly 'informational' is an assumption that analysis can soon explode. For the purposes of 'informing', a simulacrum can be every bit as good as the real thing, as every teacher and trainer knows; and we have to suspect that the demand for 'authentic' artefacts in this context is somehow, and by subterranean channels, connected to the demand for the authentic presence of the artist in the signed, unique work of art – what Walter Benjamin referred to as the aesthetic 'aura'. This is nothing to do with 'information' or archaeology, and a great deal to do with cultural expectations and ideology. That is to say, with taste.

A person of my own expectations is offended by the promiscuous and imperfectly acknowledged mixing of authenticity and simulation; but I suspect that persons younger than myself are not so offended. These are differences of taste, not categorical difficulties. No-one is being deceived.

c) Visualisation

The mode of visualisation provides us with very important clues to the nature of this whole experience. The mode is that of the sublime. In particular, sublimity as evoked by the very ancient, by the ancestral and the archaic. And in more particularity still by the ancestral as being 'Celtic', not to mention 'Ossianic' in its afflatus.

With that in mind, it was not surprising to find photographs that represented the site, and its adjacent sites, as empty, quasi-sacred places filled with a silvery mist and devoid of human presence – yet speaking of the human world by its absence. Nor is it surprising that the graphic manner of 'The Other World' (created by or under the direction of Centre Screen Productions Ltd of Manchester), derives from the colour sketches of Turner and Cozens and exploits the splattering techniques of Jackson Pollock – a modern master of sublimity. Turner's 'colour beginnings' are highly relevant material; it

32. See Cook, Pat 'The Real Thing; Archaeology and Popular Culture', *CIRCA*, 56 March/April 1991, pp. 26–8.

33. Baudrillard, J. *Simulacra and Simulation*, trans. Fraser. (Ann Arbour, Univ. of Michigan 1994), esp. ch. 1.

was the artist's practice in the later stages of his career to begin a canvas or a watercolour with abstract washes of pigment of no very clear pictorial character, and then, by a process of inventive exploration, create an image out of the formlessness. These later paintings were frequently of the most extreme and fantastic sublimity – an imagery of sea monsters, wrecks and mythical figures. The use of soft-focus and stopped-frame images in the filmed parts of the presentation have a similar effect.

The 'other-worldly' images created by these means are those of *outre* neo-romanticism. There are wild mists and mountains, sunsets, lakes and forests, and the human and animal characters are suitably adapted to this scenery. Dogs and warriors are supernaturally fierce and brave, maidens (and even warrior queens) beautiful and doe-eyed beyond the demands of verisimilitude. Blood, and there's a lot of blood, is very red and expressionistically splattered. And very good fun it is.

Human and animal imagery of this kind has a long pre-history, beginning perhaps with Mannerism and Fuseli (who deserves the original credit for Superman and all subsequent superheroes) and continuing down through Wagner's original productions, the paintings of Gustave Moreau (another man for 'colour beginnings'), symbolism, and the illustrators of art nouveau and the Celtic revival, finally culminating, alas, in our own school of Jim Fitzpatrick and the illustrators of Marvel Comix.

Inserted into this is a further layer of imagery drawn from what I term the 'technological sublime' – the imagery of films such as Kubrick's *2001* and subsequent science-fiction fantasies – images of vastness depicted with geometrical simplicity. This is strongly evident in the recurrent images of sunrise, and in the spinning fiery disc that announces the story of Deirdre. There are also treatments of imagery, mixings and juxtapositions which owe a good deal to the painterly treatment of film in *Bladerunner* (directed by Ridley Scott) and similar recent productions. Furthermore, the actual technology of 'The Other World' is a miniature version of the grandiose light shows and spectacles of major rock concerts – themselves derived from the spectacular political displays of Russian futurism and the Speer/Riefenstahl rituals at Nuremberg. The link to the present day being the son-et-lumiere shows devised in the late fifties by French designers for 'heritage' purposes.

The essential point I am making is that the mode of visualisation employed in 'The Other World', and at other points in the centre, is that of the sublime, descending via Friedrich and Turner, through Wagner and late symbolism, into the nexus of political rally and mass entertainment characteristic of the twentieth century. This sublimity is reinforced by the character of the building itself – a naturalised primitivism combined with geometrical simplicity in the manner of Boullée. (For a short discussion of the architecture of J.E. Boullée and others, see below, where the topic of primitivism and sublimity in architecture arises during my fourth case study – Ceide Fields Centre.)

The question is now – what does this mean? What does it mean for the visitor's experience of an archaeological site to have its imaginative representation (rather than its data) visualised in terms of the sublime; and what does this imply for a study of cultural tourism in Ireland?

Looked at in the larger frame of history and present policy, Ireland has always been represented to the tourist in terms of the sublime. Like the Highlands of Scotland, like Brittany and the Alps and other regions, Ireland (especially its western coast) has stood for the primitive, the unspoilt, the wild and the natural. The history of this has been well understood and investigated by a number of writers. Ossianic frauds and spurious traditions mixed with real scholarship and archaeology are major features in the representation of these regions (as noted above in chapter 3). There is nothing new about the 'promiscuity' of the visitors centre.

And Ireland continues to be 'sold' as the site of the sublime, as well as of the picturesque. The cultural tourist looks for the cultural experience, and the tourist agency provides it. This is no less true of the six counties of Northern Ireland, though north of the border it has been difficult to maintain with a straight face.

In his study 'Tourism, Public Policy and the Image of Northern Ireland since the Troubles', David Wilson has analysed the relation between the rate of 'terrorist incidents' and the rate and nature of tourist visits, and the way in which these are categorised and presented in government reports.[34] The entire question is a good deal more complex than might at first seem likely, and includes an element of morbid curiousity. The response of the Northern Ireland Tourist Board to the difficulties it has encountered has been to promote 'special interest' holidays. Historical and architectural interests are seen as notably important, and it is in this context that the visitors centre needs to be considered. The centre is, moreover, only one element in a very ambitious plan to turn Armagh city into a major tourist venue.

I forebear to comment on the economic assumptions that underlie this project, except to say that a reliance on tourism can never be anything but shaky, and that, in creating low, rather than high-skilled employment, the tourist industry may actually disable the local population and reproduce a form of servant class. But the resources employed are, I think, important. The finance for the visitors centre,

34. See Wilson, D., 'Tourism, Public Policy and the Image of Northern Ireland since the Troubles', in O'Connor and Cronin (eds.) (1993), ch. 7.

and for the other Armagh attractions, comes from a mixture of local and national government (that is, ultimately, the Northern Ireland Office), through tourist agencies, and from the European Union and the International Fund for Ireland. These are all forces working toward the normalisation of Ulster (a notion that is itself highly problematic), yet they have chosen the least 'normal' of all possible modes – the sublime – as the primary mode of visualisation and architectural image. This is a curious and apparently contradictory rhetorical strategy. What does it mean for the possibilities of this kind of popular history? What might it tell us about Ulster's 'normalisation'?

The first effect is to deepen the gap between the 'real' and the 'other' worlds. This gap, already sketched out in 'The Dawning', becomes the major feature of the whole final experience, because it is not possible to assimilate the real archaeological and historical interest of the one, to the neo-epic imagery of the other.

This was not necessary. Using the same methods, the epic material could and, we may feel, should, have been critically developed using the 'promiscuous mingling' employed with success in the 'real' archaeological section. The device of the commentator/narrator is already being used to undercut the epic afflatus, with humour. Let us suppose it used a little further, with genuinely researched questions being asked. What was the role of cattle rustling and selective breeding in ancient societies? How were military castes selected and trained? What basis has the *Táin* cycle in more than legendary history? What might some of the more obscure elements of the story actually mean? Where are the real sites of these legendary events? Perhaps most important of all; does the separation of Ulster from the rest of Ireland have deep geo-political and ethnic foundations?

These are all questions that could have been developed within the 'promiscuous' methods of the centre as a whole, and within the format of the 'Other World'. But, and this is surely a crux point, not as 'other-worldly', but as returning the epic to its true 'this-worldly' status as an ancient form of popular history, an imaginary representation comprehensible and critically available to all. The form appropriate to a pre-literate society, whose power is not diminished but actually increased when it is viewed as such.

The failure to look critically at the epic (as opposed to the questioning of the archaeological evidence), the insistence on a separation of worlds, is a mark of a profound imaginative and cognitive problem; the difficulty we find in reconciling two forms of knowledge. And its effect is to represent history as sublime.

This is a problem that has immediate consequences. The imagery of romantic sublimity – evoked by the Celtic revival, and more particularly by Yeats and Pearse, is once again contested ground. The woes of Ulster are represented to the world as spectacle and are even, most insidious of all, experienced by ourselves in that mode. The imagery of paramilitary violence thrives on such unacknowledged ambiguities and a taste for the sublime. Its opposite, utilitarian moralism, is no less available to ideological manipulation. We may view the antagonistic rhetorics of 'terrorism' versus 'self-determination', 'law and order' versus 'the freedom-fighter' as epiphenomenon of this problem. Neither, as rhetorics, are adequate for an understanding of the situation. Meanwhile the body-count and the racketeering. I see little chance of these rhetorics being replaced unless there is a sustained and intellectually adequate analysis of their origins, 'peace-processes' notwithstanding. With this in mind, we wonder at the naïvety of the scriptwriters of 'The Other World'.

As for cultural tourism and special interest holidays, seen now as part of a strategy of 'normalisation' promoted by outside agencies, what does this critical failure imply? Well, it seems from what I have argued that nothing is to change; that the chasm between fact and fancy is being inscribed, in this instance, into the very project of normalisation by way of the tourist attraction and 'heritage'. And with that inscription, the inability to rethink deep questions of identity and reality, and therefore legitimacy, which can only be done by bringing an equal critical force to bear both upon the data of history and its imaginative representation. As represented by 'The Other World', the normalisation offered us is one of a de-problematised sublimity and collective amnesia.

Is this what we want? When the imaginative representation of the North is a matter of life and death, I don't think we can insist too strongly on the relation between imaginative representation and the problem of legitimacy. Without their alignment, civil society is not possible. And this is preceded by the critical task of aligning the data of history with its representation. This is a task that the spectacle of 'The Other World' refuses.

Now you may object that I am producing an elephantine critical cannon to shoot a small and entertaining mouse. But if we are to discuss heritage and cultural tourism, we have to discuss the nature of imaginative representations, because such tourism is a pursuit of representations; and these representations have a necessary and dynamic relationship to questions of history and legitimacy. They are not in an 'other world', but in this world, with real consequences. The separation of cognitive worlds at the visitors centre is not a small matter; it divorces imagination from reason, in the name of a normalising 'heritage'. But we have to create whole minds. I described this as a critical task, but more closely considered, such an enterprise is an ethical and imaginative endeavour. And this, in brief, is why the topics of 'heritage' and cultural tourism, coming together as bearers and formers of popular history and the imaginative representation of the state, deserve our close attention.

I think, too, that it will be clear that although we have been discussing an extreme example, the issues raised here are not the exclusive preserve of Northern Ireland.

This consideration of the role of the sublime leads naturally to my next example.

4. Ceide Fields Centre, Co. Mayo

> As we look today at the great expanse of modern unbroken bogland it is hard to imagine that a second very different landscape is present beneath the blanket of bog. Ceide Fields is this second landscape that exists in exactly the same place but now lies buried under anything up to four metres of bog. It is separated from us today, not just by metres of bog but by five thousand years of time. . . . The experience of walking again in these ancient fields which have been buried for almost fifty centuries – that is what Ceide Fields is about. (Office of Public Works brochure 1995)

The concept of the sublime is, as we have seen, to be treated with caution; it leads toward a deformation of historical response by glorifying the extreme, the desperate and the violent; even, ultimately, death. But are there occasions when sublimity is an appropriate mode of response, because great antiquity and the origins of social life are what we are called upon to witness?

The question is raised by an analysis of the Ceide Fields Centre, Co. Mayo. This is a building created by the Office of Public Works near Ballina on the north coast of Co. Mayo at a particularly bleak and sublime spot where, some years ago, very ancient field patterns were discovered. These fields and the associated dwellings and artefacts show without doubt that the civilised (or at least, agrarian) history of Ireland, and therefore the islands of the North Atlantic as a whole, is substantially older than had been hitherto estimated. There is good evidence to show a milder climate, decent levels of cultivation and a settlement of peoples who had come either by land or sea to a place that is now almost abandoned. As the official brochure says:

> When we look at a normal landscape today and try to visualise in the mind's eye what it was like fifty centuries ago we probably imagine a wilderness of forest and mountain showing little human impact . . . [but] . . . Here we have the very opposite where the ancient is the lived-in land and the modern is the wilderness.

As you drive along the coast road travelling west from Ballina, you pass through the small town of Ballycastle (one of those Irish towns that seems to have no very clear reason for being where they are), and take a long hill that climbs across a shoulder of high ground. A wonderful coast appears in view, of bays and cliffs and stacks against which, on a rough day, immense waves will be breaking. At the top of this hill the road turns inland into a small valley and across the valley, exactly opposite, you see outlined against the sky, a pyramid. It is hard to tell just how large this structure is, because the land is without any other feature except the pyramid and the road. Long slopes of turf descend steadily, without interruption, to the edge of immense vertical sea cliffs.

On arrival, the pyramid seems quite small. One side of the building is almost buried in earth, and it is topped with a glass belvedere which can be reached from outside by a railed path that spirals up three of the four faces. A sloped way leads up to a ceremonious entrance: one must first pass through a circular 'court' with high turf sides.

Several allusions are built into this approach: the great pyramids themselves (not just those in Egypt, but those in numerous ancient sites around the globe), the ceremonial avenue, the ante-chamber of a court grave, Bernini's circular piazza before St Peter's, and the gates of death itself. The pyramid is made of exactly cut and smoothed silvery-black limestone blocks, repetitious and uniform. This is a small example of the sublime in architectural shape; the combination of the bleak site, the vast cliffs below and the stark symmetry of the building remind us, forcefully, that

> The irresistibility of the might of nature forces upon us the recognition of our physical helplessness as beings of nature, but at the same time reveals a faculty of estimating ourselves as independent of nature, and discovers a pre-eminence above nature that is the foundation of a self-preservation of quite another kind. . . .[35]

35. Kant, I. *Critique of Judgement* 28, 11, trans. Meredith (Oxford, Clarendon Press 1952 edn.).

Physical grandeur, antiquity and death are brought together in a single, simple and very ancient architectural image. We are confronted with an archetype.

When we enter through the heavy swinging doors, we find ourselves in a space a great deal larger than we had expected; much of the building is underground. We see in front of us an array of pillars holding up an interior gallery which forms a circle within the square plan. Standing on the ground floor and penetrating through the gallery stands an enormous piece of bog-timber – a pine tree trunk. Its bright ochre contrasts with the sandstone, grey and metal sheens of the other materials, and the warmer tints of paintwork.

There is an information desk, a well-designed refreshment area with handsome chairs and tables and, to the left, an exhibition

5.35 Approach to Céide . . .

5.36

5.37

5.38

5.39

5.40

5.42

5.41

space. The details of the wood and steelwork are very carefully executed, to an extremely high standard. In the further right-hand corner is a small but well-planned lobby containing a screen, projection booth and a slope of seats. A stairway leads up from beside the refreshment area to the gallery. The gallery has a steel and polished wood rail all round it, and the top of the pine tree rises up through a circular opening in the floor, also railed.

There are cases containing geological exhibits. From this gallery the stair continues, curving at first and then taking a right-angled leap skyward into the belvedere. This stair now resembles an expensively crafted fire-escape, and it is not a place for the nervous because it is steep and seems to fall away directly beneath you to the floor of the pyramid.

It leads past some massive steelwork – which gives a touch of the technological sublime to this ancient form – into a small square upper gallery from which you can look out over the coastline and the hillside. You can then pass out through a tiny double-doored lobby, rather like an air-lock, onto an outer balcony. To do this on a day of high winds is an exhilarating experience. Thence you descend the spiral stepped ramp round three sides of the pyramid, admiring the precision of its stonework. Each step represents a century of time, so that the final step is five thousand years ago, and we are at the point where we can re-enter once more into the ancestral vault.[36] Or you can walk or be guided up the hillside behind the centre and inspect the unearthed traces of old walls; white stones poke through the dark brown turf.

36. The Ceide Fields Centre received a Regional Award from the RIAI in 1994, and an AAI Award for Excellence in the same year. Office of Public Works architects are formally anonymous, but the AAI award was accepted on behalf of the office by Mary MacKenna.

The symbolism of this narrative is clear enough and, despite the small scale of the building, powerful: death, resurrection, enlightenment, return. To encounter the origins we have to encounter the end of life.

There is, of course, a long architectural history of such symbolism, beginning far back with grave structures of the most primitive kind, evolving into the major building projects of the ancient world. The symbolism of geometrical simplicity was revived during the eighteenth century as part of the cult of the sublime, under the influence of neo-classicism and the new physics. For Galileo, geometrical simplicity is the key to our understanding of the universe, because

> It is written in mathematical language; the characters are triangles, circles, and other geometrical figures, without which it is impossible to understand a single word: without these there is only aimless wandering in a dark labyrinth.[37]

37. Galilei, G. *Opere V* trans. Brophy and Paolucci (New York, Burns and MacEachern 1962), p. 232.

Christopher Wren translated this directly into a theory of architectural expression in which 'natural or geometrical beauty' was the highest:

'Geometrical figures are naturally more beautiful than other irregular; in this all consent as to a law of nature . . . etc.'[38]

During the later part of the eighteenth century, buildings and monuments were designed and sometimes built that embodied this extreme simplicity. John Aislabie, of Studley Royal, caused a large wooden pyramid to be constructed at the end of the avenue leading up from the house to where Burges's church now stands, as a memorial to his father. J. Etienne Boullée, (in 1784) under the influence of the theory of sublimity, designed a grandiose monument to Isaac Newton in the form of a vast hollow sphere, pierced with holes to portray the starry heavens and all their constellations to those who entered the inner darkness. Other precedents can be found in the design of mausolea and follies.[39] The idea passes into the twentieth century through le Corbusier's insistence that a massive simplicity of form is one of the 'constants of expression'.[40] The Ceide Fields Centre is a small but entirely consistent descendant of that lineage.

Such a symbolism is, necessarily, ahistoric and takes away our attention from the ordinary, archaeological *fact* of our predecessors (an ordinariness which the literature emphasises) and leads it toward an appraisal of their *extremity*. Taken further (though I doubt if this is intended) we are invited to enter into an archaic and cyclical time-structure. To cite Eliade again:

> the crucial difference between the man of the archaic civilizations and modern, historical man lies in the increasing value the latter gives to historical events . . . that, for traditional man, represented meaningless conjunctures or infractions of norms . . . The man who adopts the historical viewpoint would be justified in regarding the traditional conception of archetypes and repetition as an aberrant re-identification of history with nature. Archaic man's rejection of history, his refusal to situate himself in a concrete, historical time would, then, be the symptom of . . . fear . . .[41]

The historically conscious human being of today confronts the ancient past with a gesture that embraces and therefore transcends the death that the most ancient phenomena always thrust into our consciousness; and does so by invoking the archetypal tomb.

Of course, the everyday visitor coming as tourist or scholar will not always comprehend this symbolism immediately or directly; but I do not think it is possible to visit the centre without sensing an 'atmosphere'. It is a powerful building that draws our attention forcibly toward its object (though we are not quite certain what that object is). Are we celebrating the origins of social life, or contemplating death? If the first, is this grandiosity appropriate?

At present, the site is still rather raw, and the replanting of heather and reseeding with grass is still in progress: but when that has been

38. Wren, C. *Parentalia* (1750). For discussion, see J.A. Bennett, 'Christopher Wren: the Natural Causes of Beauty', *Architectural History* 15, 1972 pp. 5–22.

39. An introduction to this area can be made through *Architecture in the Age of Reason: Baroque and Post-Baroque in England, Italy and France* by Emil Kaufmann (Cambridge Mass., Harvard UP 1955, Archon Books 1966 repr.). Etienne-Louis Boullée (1728–1799) was seeking to balance both romantic and rationalist impulses, while seeking a new architectural style. With other architects of the immediately pre-revolutionary period he experimented with the boldest possible use of primary geometric shapes. Few of his buildings were in fact completed, and he exists in architectural history as a magnificent draughtsman, creating images that echo through the collective unconscious of the profession. See also work by Ledoux, Hawksmoor, Sobre and others.

40. See Ozenfant, A. *The Foundations of Modern Art* (New York, Dover Publ. 1952 edn.), and le Corbusier *Towards a New Architecture*, trans. Etchells, 9th edn. (Architectural Press, London 1970).

41. Eliade, op. cit., p. 154–5.

completed, and the structure half-naturalised back into the soil from which it appears to rise, the image and the narrative will be impressive.

The principal *visualisation* involved in the centre is the video film that is shown at regular intervals in the lobby.[42] This is a well-crafted piece, taking us through the geological structures of the north Mayo coast, through the erosions of millennia, through glacial planishing and, at last, into the realm of human history. It cannot resist making an appeal to the sublime because any depiction of wild coastlines, vast waves, and any evocation of geological time cannot but engender a sense of awe in a modern sensibility. We are ourselves constructed through our cultural expectations to be susceptible to these scenes; that is what it is like to be us. The film is entitled *Written in Stone* and the text begins with a poem by Séamus Heaney; there are references to 'stepping back in time' and (of course!) mention of 'the great Celtic peoples'. The sound track makes use of 'traditional' music spliced with crashing waves and synthesised drum rolls.

Through the film we learn about the unusual geological collisions and confusions of the coast, about the insecurity of the cliffs, about the indentations, creeks, caves and blowholes and, at length, something about the conditions under which our predecessors lived. We learn that north Mayo is a much degraded human environment, that it once supported a rich vegetation, with great pine trees; and that what we see now is something like a disaster area. Was this the fault of our predecessors, who did not know how to manage the clearing of forest and so, in time, brought down the bog upon themselves? (And we can't help reflecting upon the latter-day consequences of subsistence farming and monoculture, of peasant economies leading to famine and to depopulation, and to the stranding of little towns like Ballycastle that now seem to be much larger than warranted.)

There is now a wealth of accumulated experience in this sort of film-making, learnt mainly through treatment of wildlife and popular science topics. It is a definite genre, which we recognise and understand. While purists may object to the 'sublime' elements and the romantic drama, this writer does not; I take the view (which of course is not easily substantiated) that the conventions of the genre are well understood by the usual visitors, who take away from the film an understanding that has genuinely been increased. The rhetoric is understood as rhetoric, and enjoyed for its own sake. (Compare, for example, the anthropomorphism of many wildlife programmes.) The usual visitor has, where films of this kind are concerned, a great deal of viewing experience, and extensive tacit knowledge of its allurements. Far more experience of the seductions of film than of the manipulations of architecture.

42. The film *Written in Stone* is directed by Leo Carey with script by Séamus Caulfield.

The craftsmanship of the film is not, unfortunately, carried over into the exhibition area, where there is a dismal simulation of ancient life in the form of huts, dummies, artefacts, and murals, some of which are wretchedly bad. But given that *simulation* is a constant feature of the heritage idea, what might have been the reality that could best be exhibited here? The centre offers the opportunity for a truly interesting investigation. The official brochure asks the question 'Were these people Celts?' (despite the film commentary) and answers 'Definitely not. And then again, maybe yes.' There is, we learn, an intricate argument about their origins, which is still unresolved. Briefly, for these people to have been Celts (i.e. speakers of some recognisable early Celtic tongue), then the spread of farming methods and the spread of the Indo-European languages had to have been linked. The difficulty with this is that it forces us to revise the dating of the spread of the languages to a much earlier time than has been generally accepted.

The mythologically inclined amongst us are likely to think of legendary forebears, Firbolgs, Fomorians and the Tuatha Dé Danann, as imagined traces of aboriginal inhabitants, squashed down under the subsequent arrivals. Have we, in excavating the Ceide Fields, dug them up again into the light of archaeology and science? The nature of the earliest inhabitants is always worth pursuing, because accounts of them are always a part of the definition of the latest, and the question of who or what is 'Celtic' (not to mention 'Irish') is certainly not a neutral question. The origin of a people is always, as the sixteenth-century antiquarian William Camden wrote 'confounded with fabulous conjectures'. It is a nexus around which concepts of race, nationality, history and culture continually circle; and in this case it is also a part of the continued construction of Ireland as a place that European tourists must visit. Ireland's claims to Celticity are now part of a major industry – that we would hesitate to upset. Major economic interests are at stake. Nevertheless, here is a real question that we might have expected the exhibition to unpick, though we may doubt if such an enquiry is best conducted in a tomb.

Chapman comes very close to describing the 'Celts' as *merely* the products of a discourse which continues to ascribe to 'peripheral' peoples certain qualities; to describe oneself as 'Celtic' would be, in such an argument, to will one's own subjection.[43] But there is a real and material distinction between how objects are named and what in fact they are. Given the logical inconsistencies and the unsustainable racism by which notions of the 'Celtic' were first constructed in modern times, there remains the fact that many people, which includes most Irish, wish to identify themselves as Celtic; and there are phenomena to which the term has been consistently applied. There is

43. See esp. Chapman op. cit., p. 251–65.

a family of languages that we call Celtic because peoples we call 'Celtic' speak them; even if the relation between the speakers of Celtic languages and the 'Celts' need be no closer than the relation that exists between speakers of English and the 'English'. Likewise, there exists a consistent body of art and craftwork that we call Celtic art, even if, as it developed through time, we have to keep qualifying it as 'Hiberno-Saxon' or 'insular'. These are real and concrete phenomena, produced by real and concrete persons and, in principle, questions about them are decideable because they are within the same logical categories; but how 'Celtic art' maps onto 'Celtic languages' and the peoples known as 'Celts' is a very obscure and messy affair indeed.

We have to avoid the error of assuming that, because we have given certain phenomena the same adjectival noun, they are in fact the same. The name is a product of the discourse, not of the reality; and one must not mistake the one for the other. The position this writer takes is that study of language, art, and human geography under the heading 'Celtic' is fine so long as we don't assume a transcending and unifying identity between the three fields; because that assumption is part of the nineteenth-century identification of culture with language and race and nation. There may be an identity, but it may tell us no more than speaking English, assembling Japanese electronics and living in Carrickfergus tells us about 'Irish identity'. Identity, in this sense, has almost nothing to do with attributes and almost everything to do with volition. *The identity that matters is the one we choose for ourselves.* So the question arises – do we claim these ancient peoples as our kindred; and what do we mean by so doing?

This touches on the foundations of popular history; moreover not only an Irish popular history, but the common popular history of the islands at large. I write these words in a city that has no common popular history, that consists of separate cognitive realms and defended spaces, without norms, where horrible crimes continue to be committed for the sake of 'identity'; in a happier vein I write as one whose maternal forebears came from Mayo and who identifies himself as 'British' (rather than 'English'), and I write as one who feels a sense of awe as I encounter the traces of this ancient people.

There is an essay by Goethe on granite, in which the poet describes himself laying his hand upon a rock that he knows reaches down into the fiery heart of the world; that granite is an absolute. And in that frame of mind, laying my hand upon the ancient inhabitants of the Ceide Fields, I ask myself just what sort of exhibition or display would bring out some of these questions.

If this imagined exhibition were to claim that the people of Ceide were, in some sense, 'Celts', then it would moderate the notion of 'Celticism'. The people of Ceide were methodical, industrious, well-organised and peaceful – indeed, they were the very anti-type of everything that has been generally attributed to 'Celts'. This is not a small matter. It might even be incorporated into a revised and modernised popular history, that would make of 'Ireland' an unexceptional part of the wider European history; a place that was nowhere special. It might even go some small way toward creating a common popular history where none now exists, and without which political legitimacy in the future may be as shaky as it has been in the past.

Conversely, if this exhibition were to argue the contrary case, or leave a decision on the matter up to its visitors, we would still have to revise 'Celticity' because the 'Celts' could no longer claim to be aboriginally Irish. Compared with Ceide Fields, who is not another 'blow-in'? And it would be a refusal of the example of constructive co-operation which these people offer us.

The Office of Public Works, as an agent of the state, needs to be clear in its orientation. As the Ceide Fields Centre now stands, it is not sufficiently clear just what or whom is being celebrated or explicated, or why. There is an opportunity here to develop an exhibition devoted to these questions, that would qualify the architectural sublimity with dispassionate enquiry. Without that, this impressive building is no more than a rhetorical gesture directed at nothing clearly defined.

What this may tell us about the cultural policies of the Haughey administration, under whose aegis the building was proposed, would be part of another enquiry. Nothing could be more different in its studious avoidance of rhetoric than our next example. The question of a common popular history, what it might be and how it might operate, hangs heavily over my next and final example.

5. The Famine Museum, Strokestown, Co. Roscommon

> The Great Irish Famine of the 1840s was the single greatest catastrophe of 19th century Europe. Between 1845 and 1850, when blight devastated the potato crop, one quarter of the Irish population – in excess of two million people – either died or emigrated. The modern period in Ireland flows from a deathly origin which unmade the Irish nation and scattered it across the globe. . . . The museum uses the extensive Strokestown archive, both to explain the significance of this tragic event nationally, and to reflect on the ongoing spectacle of contemporary global poverty and hunger . . . By preserving the estate and by establishing the Famine Museum, the Westward Group have 'restored' the property in one important respect. Strokestown Park now assumes a new and meaningful significance in an Ireland radically different to the one which originally produced it.[44]

44. From *The Great Irish Famine: Words and Images from the Famine Museum* by Stephen Campbell, The Famine Museum, Strokestown (1994).

The Famine Museum, in the grounds of Strokestown Park House, is in all respects the opposite of the preceding example, but an analysis of the museum by itself is rather difficult, because the experience it offers is contained in the wider experience of visiting the whole park and the house.[45] My initial analysis must therefore be followed by a broader treatment that places the first within the second.

(For readers who are not Irish it is important to understand that the Great Famine of the 1840s simultaneously destroyed and created. An old Ireland either died or fled abroad and a new one, with modern class relations, railways, administration and language replaced it. Accounts of this terrible period have always tended toward two extremes – a 'nationalist' agenda that has used the events to support its own imperatives, and a more recent 'revisionist' school that has looked much more closely at the modernising consequences and drawn different conclusions. Each was driven by ideological requirements, and the first case can be read as a self-justifying argument by those who had, in class terms, benefited from the re-organisation of land-use that followed. Much more recently, studies of the Famine have seen it in terms of the famine phenomenon as a whole, looking for an approach that can amalgamate the Irish experience with other great hungers in recent history. The historiography of the Famine, at both the popular and scholarly levels, is an extremely loaded topic.[46] But the really striking fact, for our purposes here, is that there has been no public memorial, museum or any substantial commemoration in the century and a half since. The Strokestown Famine Museum, created by private individuals, is the only institution of its kind.)

The museum is contained in an outbuilding of the house – a long L-shaped structure along two sides of a walled courtyard. This building is partly restored and partly new-built in the same manner and was designed by Orna Hanley for the Westward Trust. It is an architecture completely without rhetoric, except insofar as to refuse the grand gesture is itself a persuasive device.

We pass through a series of very simple stone and concrete spaces linked by plain doorless gaps, and lit with great simplicity. There are a number of simple but elegant display cases and stands and several arrays of boards containing text and imagery. On the wall are prints and photographs, but never very many. There are a small number of objects. Visually, this is a sparse environment. It is, I believe, significant that the design of the lighting, the cases and stands was done by the architect; there is a satisfying unity here which is completely lacking in the Ceide Fields exhibition area.

The narrative topology of these rooms is straightforwardly chronological and one-way. We learn about the potato, its introduction from

45. This difficulty has been noted by Niall Ó Cíosáin in an article for *CIRCA*, to which I am indebted. See 'Hungry Grass' in *CIRCA*, 68 Summer 1994, pp. 24–7.

46. See ch. 2, note 53; and also Poirtéir C. (ed.) *The Great Irish Famine; The Thomas Davis Lecture Series* (Dublin, RTÉ/Mercier 1995).

5.43 An architecture without rhetoric – Famine Museum buildings, Strokestown House.

the New World, the growing dependence of the Irish peasantry upon it and the social structures that floated upon that dependence. There is useful political and economic information on the boards and a fine display of political cartoons. We learn about farming methods and land-use (a particularly clear and elegant model is used); and we are invited in passing to set the Irish Famine in the wider context of contemporary hungers. Then we learn of the blight, the start of the Famine, the British government's attempts at famine-relief through poor-law enactments and workhouses, about the abandonment of that relief under the dual pressure of its practical insufficiency and theories of free markets, and about the catastrophe that then ensued. We see a short film and hear a commentary. In the penultimate section we learn of the assassination of the owner of the Strokestown estate, and the spread of secret societies; finally we are confronted with some of the consequences – a legacy of political instability, of the decay of a language, of modernisation by default. Thence we pass through to a small bookshop and into a well-appointed restaurant where we can eat well while thinking about those who ate nothing.

In this respect, the museum has the directed one-way narrative of a rather old-fashioned didactic exhibition; but that narrative is continually undercut by visual and auditory commentaries that emphasise the lack of knowledge, the obscurity of the historical material, and the one-sidedness of any possible story that can draw no evidence from the dead and gone. Almost all the available material on the Famine is provided by those *who did not go hungry*. It is also the case that the exhibition is constantly evolving and changing in its details, as the curator (Luke Dodd) and his team circulate documents from the archives and additional material as their own understanding of the Famine develops.

The commentary consists of contemporary evidence and is also about and rests upon that evidence. This is a strategy of some sophistication, which demands a high level of attention from visitors; it is executed in a manner that owes much to the practices of contemporary conceptual artists. Indeed, a number of artists have been involved directly in the creation of the museum and this shows in the very acute and critical attitude to display and visualisation, which photographs cannot clearly reproduce. For this reason I have not included illustrations of the interior of the Famine Museum.

It is also necessary to amend my three headings to take account of the spoken voice.

Audio Commentary

A continuing feature of the experience as we walk through the rooms is the sound of voices, reading softly, muttering or whispering. These are the voices of contemporary writers, eye-witnesses, keepers of journals and compilers of reports. Discreet loudspeakers, some almost invisible, relay their messages to us from an un-enterable space. Sometimes these voices are female, reading material that we know to have been written by men. The strangest are those that administer the oaths of secret societies and tell us, through contemporary accounts, of the murder of Major Mahon; these are sometimes hardly audible, so we have to pay close attention. These texts are not acted out, but offered as verbal objects which *we* have to fit into the frame provided by the physical evidence and the imagery (which is itself trying hard *not* to tell an obvious story). Thus we become, whether or not we intend it, participants in the creation of the narrative.

Visual Commentary

This consists mainly of enlarged political cartoons and illustrations from the *Illustrated London News*, as well as maps and models and charts. The cartoons tell their own story and hardly need commentary; but the illustrations are given an interesting gloss, since they repeat picturesque assumptions about the peasantry and the conventions of depiction are being used to mediate the raw experience of the catastrophe with art-historical references. There are also a number of archival photographs and at least one very telling image of two modern photographers crouching beside a hungry African child as they look for the best 'angle of shot'. Hardly anything could show more clearly the position of superiority that visual evidence nearly always embodies than this photograph; the poor make no pictures.

Both visual and auditory commentary come together in a short film made by the artist Pat Murphy. This is a beautiful piece in which we see an empty workhouse and empty fields under an empty sky, and whose imagery is intercut with a text that never exactly matches the image on the screen so that there is a 'delayed action' effect on our understanding. This delayed action or continuous off-set of information frustrates any conventional narrative and is, in effect, a simulation of the real experience of *doing history*,[47] in which no evidence ever quite matches the frame we have been forming for it and into which we are hoping it will fit. We are quietly compelled to assess the evidence and think for ourselves, as if we were, in Topolski's terms, surveying the evidence both forward and back, as scholars.

In setting up this self-critical method, however, the museum has opened itself up to a further level of critical analysis. This can be seen in its own commentary upon the visual evidence that it has assembled from the pages of the *Illustrated London News*. Since this raises an important problem of interpretation, it is necessary to diverge somewhat from my previous method and study the original material rather than its manner of display.

These woodcuts, which are by far the most substantial *visual* record of the Famine, are presented both as evidence of the Famine, and as evidence of British attitudes to Irish suffering. The captions draw attention to the stereotypical poses of dejection and regard them as indicating stereotypical 'colonial' attitudes. While not entirely dissenting from this (the privileged position of the picturesque having been established in chapter 3), I think a serious analysis has to go much further. We are looking at the use made of representations, as well as the representations themselves.

At its simplest level, this is how one depicted suffering, *any suffering*, in 1847; and this is how one depicted peasants, *any peasants*. It would not be hard to find similar images of peasants anywhere, hungry or not; and we have already noted how 'colonial' attitudes could come to be, later, the stock-in-trade of nationalists. The three artists whose names are recorded were all Irish and all from Cork.

Reproduced in the exhibition is the painting *The Discovery of the Potato Blight in Ireland* by Daniel McDonald (1821–1853), where a family, opening their store, take up classical attitudes of dejection and despair; behind them a picturesque landscape is being overtaken by a sublime thunder-cloud, and an old man raises his eyes to heaven in an Ossianic fervour.[48] The original title of the painting was much more descriptive and 'realist': *An Irish Peasant Family Discovering the Blight of Their Potato Store*. If the painting now appears highly idealised, it may not have seemed so to contemporaries.

McDonald is known to have published a print of Father Matthew, whose records of the 'Hunger' are an important primary source for historians, so we may assume McDonald to have been fully aware of

47. See my 'Introduction' above (ch. 1) for a discussion of 'doing history'.

48. Daniel McDonald (1821–53) was born in Cork, and something of an infant prodigy, publishing his first etchings at the age of thirteen.

the real conditions in west Cork, even if he was painting in Dublin. Father Matthew's report of the coming of the blight along the Cork to Dublin road (27 July 1846) is quoted frequently.

Images of this character now seem to us quite inadequate to the circumstances; not only is the disaster depicted as a natural calamity or act of God, but the victims are seen as passive. But in 1847 *there was no other way of painting peasants*. For political insight one must turn to the cartoonists of the day, such as those in *McNean's Monthly Sheets*. Here, freed from pictorial conventions, the artists and caption-writers had licence to be as inventive, accurate and sardonic as any in history.

When we turn to newspapers and journals which attempted to show what was 'really happening', there is a continuous mismatch between the real events and their depiction. But to understand the problem one must understand the process by which the imagery of the *Illustrated London News* was created, and the terms in which it was conceived.

These images are mediated by two 'filters'. In terms of visual ideology they are the late product of the picturesque. At the very time when thousands were dying, artistic visitors were being urged to go out into Connemara in search of groups of peasants that would 'furnish a striking and picturesque sketch', and would be 'accessories

5.45 J. Mahony and engravers 'Govt. Sale of Indian Corn' (1847)

5.46 J. Mahony and engravers 'Ballydehob from the Skibbereen Road' (1847)

5.47 H. Smith and engravers 'Funeral at Skibbereen' (1847) – the mix of caricature and reportage.

5.48 J. Mahony and engravers 'Boy and Girl at Cahera' (1847) the style of this engraving is markedly different from most others.

to the landscape' (see chapter 3). We have seen this attitude continue right through the century and up to the present day, perpetuated by Irish artists and photographers as much as by anyone else.

The second 'filter' was technological; the imagery in the *Illustrated London News* was the product of a chain of processes each step of which took it further from the original observational drawing, through a hierarchy of tracers, engravers and assemblers (each one of which had been trained in particular codes and conventions), toward the codes and conventions expected by a readership of a certain range – that is toward a distinct visual ideology, which tended to make everything look similar so that it is sometimes difficult to distinguish between a real-life scene and the reproduction of a painting.

We do not, generally, have the names of the originating artist-reporters, but the sufferings of the Skibbereen district in west Cork were documented by James Mahony, who sent back both image and copy to London.[49] It is reasonable to suppose that the original sketches were pen-and-wash drawings, probably with annotations for the engraver. Mahony was himself working within the conventions of the picturesque artist's sketch-book. The drawing, on arrival in London, would be subject to editorial decisions as to size, proportions and *mise-en-page*; then handed to the engravers, with instructions. These engravers were usually employed by small firms specialising in particular kinds of work; the *News* did not have engravers of its own but 'put out' work to established firms such as the Dalziel brothers, Linton and Co. and Landells. The original drawing or its reduced copy was then traced onto a block by one craftsperson before being handed on to another for engraving; if it was a large image, several blocks might be cut by several different hands (the blocks were rarely more than three inches square). Then came a stage of checking, proofing and aligning – especially when several blocks were being employed. The finished block was then delivered to the typesetter and printer for incorporation into the printing forme along with the text. At each stage the original sketch, no matter how 'raw', is being 'cooked' into the required visual convention. The result was a highly crafted image whose technology was part of the visual ideology of its time and class. Far from being 'perfect' or 'subliminal' in its communication (and the *News* prided itself on rendering scenes 'as they really have occurred'), the prints of the Famine were, *and could only be*, highly mediated, irrespective of their origin or the intention of their artists and publishers.[50] Thus, when Mahony writes of 'such scenes of misery and privation as I trust it may never again be my lot to look upon . . .' (13 Feb. and 20 Feb. 1847) his accompanying illustration, *Government Sale of Indian Corn, at Cork* is a jolly peasant dance; and 'Ballydehob from the

49. This is probably James Mahony, ARCA, 1810–1879. A watercolourist and illustrator who travelled extensively in his youth and settled in his home town of Cork in 1842. He exhibited widely, showing watercolours of Venice, Rome, Rouen and Paris until 1846 when he is recorded as going to London, where he did much work as an illustrator. He is reported as working for the *Illustrated London News*. In some accounts he may be confused with another J. Mahony who was a book illustrator. But if it is this first J. Mahony, then he must have stayed a year longer in Cork or been sent back to report by the *News*, because our Mahony was in Skibbereen in 1847. I have been unable to trace M.H. Smith. Both men are likely to have known McDonald, whose father was an engraver in Cork.

50. There is a brief and sensitive discussion of this point by Ó Ciosáin in op. cit., pp. 26–7. 'It is as though the artists had no visual language through which to show extreme emaciation, disease or degradation.'

Skibbereen Road' is a stock picturesque scene that might well have been used somewhere else with a different caption.

There is, I think, some internal evidence that the artist-reporters and engravers of the *News* knew they were up against the limits of their craft; some images of the Famine include figures drawn in a style that hovers uncomfortably between reportage and caricature – as if the artist had been looking unsuccessfully for adequate conventions, which the engravers had been unable to comprehend; others depart suddenly, but briefly, from the conventions.

A comparison can be made with a topic of similar horror – child labour. The Parliamentary Report on the Employment of Children in the Mines and Manufactures (May 1842) contained a number of illustrations of naked and harnessed children engaged at the heaviest labour in mines. Here the shock of primary industrialisation was first given visual form. In comparison with the Famine prints, these are rudimentary sketches and they remained as such when they were republished in *Bell's Penny Dispatch* and other papers (the *News* did not publish them, since it usually steered clear of contentious material. See chapter 4 above). No attempt was ever made to give these images a conventional pictorial treatment in any medium. The sketches in the report were, and remain, profoundly shocking visual documents precisely because almost no aesthetic mediation has taken place between the original drawing and the wooden block; it did not take place *because there was no available visual convention*.

To this, the post-colonial theorist will reply that these were 'English' phenomena, and so could be treated with greater 'realism'; to that I reply in turn that the mine and factory workers of Britain were far further removed than any Irish peasant (far more 'Other') because they were an unprecedented class *that had never been subject to depiction*. The depiction of child labour involved an unprecedented artistic problem.[51] In consequence, it was not pictured, and never was until well after the passing of the Factory Acts when child labour no longer existed in so violent a form.

We can also see that the Famine illustrators found it very difficult to show real emaciation. The nearest we come to true starvation is the celebrated and often reproduced drawing of 'Bridget O'Donnell and her children' by an unknown hand (but, I guess, Mahony again) as part of a series of furious and well-informed articles on 'the terror and anarchy of eviction' (Dec. 1849). Yet even here, whatever the original source drawing, the final published engraving reproduces a conventional 'colleen' whose features are suavely re-reproduced decades later by John Lavery for the bank notes of the Free State.

The extreme of incompatibility is reached in a series of anonymous articles in the summer of 1848 entitled *Excursion to the Lakes*

51. Artists have always found difficulty in drawing objects they have never before encountered. For example, Durer's woodcut of a rhinoceros or (notoriously) Leonardo's inability to *see* the forms of the viscera and reproductive organs because he did not know their functioning. The *Illustrated London News* published an illustration of a hippopotamus on June 1 1850; it is quite clear the artist and engravers were unable to comprehend its architecture and they made it look like an unusually heavy pig.

5.49a Head of Bridget O'Donnell

5.49b Head of Mrs Lavery as Cathleen ní Houlihan (profile reversed, 1923)

52. See, for example, the small exhibition on the Famine organised jointly between the Ulster Folk Park, Cultra and Trócaire; reported on by myself in *The Irish Reporter*, 19, 1995 (pp. 18–19). The visual record of the Famine deserves much closer study. In the case of the *Illustrated London News*, while there were regular and sometimes vivid and moving written reports, visual reports were sporadic and often ambiguous. Though the article 'Views of the O'Connor Property in Ireland' (10 Jan. 1846) describes the poverty and wretchedness with some passion, the actual 'views' are stock picturesque treatments of Irish villages with only one showing signs of decay. A very sharply worded article taken from the Dublin *Freeman's Journal* is reprinted but not illustrated (4 April 1846). This is succeeded on 24 April 1847 by a reproduction of a sentimental painting (*Cavan's Well* by F.W. Topham) showing a devout Irish maiden praying at a holy well. For most of 1848, Irish illustrations disappear from the pages, which are largely taken up with the European revolutions of that year (though there are still written reports). Famine illustrations are followed on 15 Sept. 1849 with a reproduction and fullsome commentary on a painting entitled *An Irish Harvest Home* 'from an original sketch by an *Irish* artist' (italics in the original). This again is followed by a furious and well-informed series of articles on 'the terror and anarchy of eviction' (15, 22, 29 Dec. 1849) accompanied by (within the terms of the day) realistic sketches of ruined villages, turf huts and the image of 'Bridget O'Donnell and her Children'. Given the fixed policy of the *News*, that it would not deal with contentious issues, its reporting of the Famine, both literary and visual, is not dishonourable, but it is very confused. This whole topic deserves much more study, since it is the prolegomena to all famine journalism since.

of Killarney which veers wildly between picturesque travel-writing and Famine reportage. The writer remarks that all the tourists present were Irish, 'though the time is coming, I hope, when they will flock from England also'. He then looks over a wall into a mass burial-pit where bones stick out of the ground: 'Some of the skulls are as white as Parian marble, others green with moss.' He witnesses a father lamenting over his daughter's coffin and scenes of terrible lamentation – and then takes us to the Gap of Dunloe with an illustration of wild mountains and a fisherman.

The problem is similar in difficulty and intensity to the problem of depicting the Shoah. To find an aesthetic category into which photographs of the death pits of Belsen could be fitted, it was and is necessary to turn to medieval images of hell. No-one has successfully made adequate modern paintings of those terrible scenes. (The nearest attempt at adequate visualisation has been, perhaps, a few of the frames from Steven Spielberg's film *Schindler's List* (1993), because it employs the same medium and organising conventions as the original documentary footage.) And the problem is linked, too, to the questionable uses of photography in the presentation of contemporary disasters. So ubiquitous have certain images become that it is possible to speak, once again, of the aestheticisation of disaster, and to speak of the 'genre' of the starving child. This is well caught by the museum in the image of the photographers, already mentioned.

My main purpose in making these more detailed observations, and engaging in what would otherwise be a digression, is to stress how closely the visual evidence of history needs to be questioned. Text-based historians are usually very bad at this because generally they have no training in or understanding of the technologies and politics of visual representation; and art historians rarely study popular or technical imagery. How much more does this apply to the designers of exhibitions? John Urry's argument, that visualisation 'distorts' and 'trivialises' history, holds good in those cases *when the nature of the representation is not critically understood and made explicit.*[52]

Considered now from the point of view of a possible popular, non-technical history (and laying aside the issue of the engravings), the strategy of the Famine Museum seems to be genuinely emancipatory in that it invites us to participate in the creation of its meanings; we become our own story-tellers, reassembling the fragments we are offered. In Topolski's terms, we are the ones that provide the final coherence and integration, and therefore the truth. And in doing so we become aware of our own position of security and privilege, and become responsible for our own response. This is an ethical challenge of some seriousness; the museum is a very quiet place.

The experience it offers, however, takes place in a setting which provides an ironic and instructive counter-narrative.

As we pass through the broad main street of Strokestown – created by one of the Mahon family as a piece of large-scale rural improvement – we enter first through a stone gateway and then, swinging along a curving drive, first see the house to our left, through trees, before the drive curves back again. This processional entry, the proportions and the siting, make us feel that the house is imposing. This is a deception: Strokestown Park House is a small semi-Palladian structure, ingenious but not grand; it is full of visual devices to make it seem much larger and richer than in fact it is, and (like many 'Anglo-Irish' houses of its kind) its symmetries and elevations are theatrical. There is also a fine walled garden we can visit, and a small park of trees and grass bisected by a hidden river in a culvert.

The house is also a very clear example of the use of circulation patterns for the purposes of class differentiation; not only is the ceremonial front of the building in the greatest contrast to the utilitarian back, but it is possible to pass from the stable wing right under the main house in a tunnel to the kitchen wing, so that the services are fully separated off from the formal rooms excepting only at the butler's pantry. The effect is to turn the main house into a stage-setting for highly formalised behaviour. A guided tour allows us to see this, though not to explore it in detail. (The nearest equivalent to this at the same scale might be Castleward House in Co. Down; there the main house is entirely separate from the service buildings and connected to them only by a tunnel.)

The Westward Trust has made the interesting decision to leave the house in the state it was left by its last inhabitants; no attempt has been made to give it an 'original' or 'authentic' interior, other than the one it has naturally acquired. It is therefore, like any house in which the same family has lived for a long time, a complicated palimpsest which requires some guidance to read. The guides have all been invited to research the history of house and family and to develop their own informal scripts; thus different visits may yield different stories. This too is a bold strategy but it depends for its success upon the guide's ability to maintain a position independent of the expectations of visitors. There is a substantial class of tourist who visit large houses to obtain a kind of vicarious social gratification, and this is revealed in the questions they ask and the pieces of knowledge that they give out. Large houses of this kind invite these responses; and in the particular case of Strokestown and the proximity of the Famine Museum they invite a complex transaction between 'normal' snobbery and anti-'English' prejudice.[53] I do not think our guide was able to resist this pressure to conform to social expectations and it may be that in time

53. I put English between quotes ' . . . ' in order to stress the oddness of ascribing 'Englishness' (whatever that is) to a class of people who, to the English, are as 'English' as Martians. There is little 'English' about Strokestown House. What I think we are looking at is the phenomenon of class insecurity, masked by an architecture of dissimulation. Similar features exist in mansions of Alabama, in French architecture in Indo China etc. The house as a stage-setting. Our guide repeated some very old and discreditable stories.

the curatorial team will wish to employ some of the same auditory techniques that it employs in the museum. The Strokestown archive is full of the most interesting and detailed material for such a purpose. And it might also be possible to introduce a visual commentary, through short video presentations like that in the museum, that would bring out the theatrical character of the house more clearly, and our willing (temporary) participation in its values. As Ó Cíosáin puts it:

> nearing the house we expect to be shown aristocratic luxury; but are shown instead the inequality of distribution underlying that luxury; moving through the museum, we sympathise with those who suffered famine and exploitation in the past and criticise those who oppressed, only to be put in the position of exploiters . . .[54]

My anxiety is that the experience of the house as most people receive it is essentially 'diversionary'; and this extends *a fortiori* to the walled garden, which is a purely pleasurable domain. The objection, of course, is not to pleasure and diversion, but to the ease with which hard-won understandings can be lost. I suspect that in their desire to avoid a central narrative of explanation, the curatorial team have opened themselves up to a reversal of interpretation; in time the 'great house' appeal of vicarious gratification will come into conflict with the participatory structure of the museum.

It will be clear from what I have written above that I admire the strategy of presentation that is employed here because it invites us to participate in the creation of an historical understanding, and that it discloses its own self-critical premises. It is not coincidental that this has been done without recourse to government funding[55] and that the Westward Trust is an essentially private and local initiative conceived, mainly financed, developed and realised by private individuals out of their own conviction and effort. It cannot then be assessed under any easy state ideological heading; but this does not mean that the museum and its strategy is devoid of an ideological position.

The intellectual positions inscribed in the strategy are those we can broadly called 'deconstructivist' and 'cultural materialist' (and those who are confident of the term may wish to call this a 'post-modernist' strategy). In recent years this has become an orthodoxy in Ireland no less than in any other intellectual culture. In Ireland it serves a valuable, but certainly ideological function of re-positioning Irish experience and history in and beyond a post-colonial condition. In some important respects it is a rejection of 'Irishness' and 'Celticity' (as ahistorical essences) in favour of an autonomous modernity. As such, it is an oppositional gesture against seventy years of official ideology and cultural nationalism. It rejects the idea of Ireland as an historically conditioned victim with a 'peripheral' mentality.

54. Ó Cíosáin, op. cit., p. 26.

55. Government funding was indirectly useful through the young people's work scheme (FÁS). Substantial aid came from EU funds. But the predominant financing has been, I understand, provided by a local haulier. The realisation of the museum and the overall strategy of presentation has been directed by Luke Dodd, the curator. A number of individuals, many from Dublin's artistic community, gave voluntary labour. The museum was formally opened by President Mary Robinson.

But this 'autonomous modernity' is an unstable entity, which serves another function – that of consolidating a relatively new professional class, with very different priorities and interests, in its struggle against an older establishment. I interpret the Famine Museum as an attempt to seek out, through its presentation of the catastrophe, an appropriate popular history that will take account of 'revisionist' interpretations of the period, that will employ the ironic methods of 'post-modernity', without any loss of the tragic sense. This would be a popular history to supersede the 'nationalist' version without loss of national feeling; and it would reflect and also promote a re-positioning of attitudes toward Britain, Europe and 'the North'. By re-positioning the past, the future is being shaped.

The difference between this undertaking and that initiated by the Office of Public Works at Ceide Fields and elsewhere is clear enough.

I find that in setting down these five case studies I have provided myself with an agenda of topics which must be brought together in conclusion. A study of the construction of 'heritage' in the terms I have set myself must entail further analysis of, amongst other matters, the relations between 'concrete, historical time' and 'mythic time'; my contention will be that a popular history necessarily partakes of both time-concepts. It will also require more thought on the relations between popular history (as I have been defining it) and the nature of political legitimacy. I have raised on several occasions a distinction between 'unproblematic or given' and 'problematic' histories, and between 'directed' and 'undirected' narratives. I have suggested obliquely that the description of the past is also a means of prescribing the present, such that popular history (and heritage as popular history) is a form of ideology; that representation of the past may even be a fantastic or fetishised form of the present.

These are all matters general to any discussion of 'heritage' and I hope that although my concrete examples are mainly Irish, the abstract principles that follow from them can be seen in much wider terms.

6

THE REPRESENTATION OF THE PAST

In an analysis of any term as extensive and vague as 'heritage' authors must concentrate upon what they can make clear at the expense of wider ambitions. Notions such as 'literary heritage' or 'Irish heritage' I leave to others and to other methods; though I suspect that the kinds of questions and arguments I have put forward above would be pertinent. Nor have I attempted to deal with some of the crasser and more commercial uses of the term. Rather than unpicking that sort of knot I have concentrated upon buildings, exhibitions and parks which have as their purpose the representation of the past.

By choosing the word 'past' to head this concluding chapter, I mean to distinguish past time from its histories, the field of study from its representations. But, as Hayden White shows, that field can only be represented if it is first prefigured in imagination as a domain with possibly representable features. This prefiguration I interpret as a commitment – there is this field and it is important. It also asserts the existence of 'figures' or categories which form the content of the field – there is this field and it contains x, y, z; and x, y, and z are important. On that basis the writing of histories and the construction of heritage can begin.

In the examples I have discussed these 'figures' or preconditions of history have been geographical/political, ethnic, religious, national, etc. categories. Thus the name 'Ulster–American Folk Park' stands as a descriptive list of the pertinent 'figures'. That there are other categories at work in this instance, more or less undisclosed, appears only on closer analysis; thus I concluded that the truer description might read 'Ulster (Presbyterian)–American Folk Park', since the term 'Ulster' was being used as simultaneously geographical and confessional. In the case of Navan Fort it seemed that two quite different kinds of categorisation were at work – the one archaeological, the other legendary, and that these two, whilst being applied on the same ostensible ground (the fort), were radically incompatible. Where my English example was concerned, the prefiguration had to be deduced from the way in which the real site had been treated – the concept 'national heritage' began to appear as a heading under which a benign national narrative had been prefigured, as a fundamental assumption necessary to an *ancien régime*.

These deep strata, or fundamental assumptions, were not themselves under question. It now seems to me, on reflection, that the idea of 'heritage' is rooted in these imaginative figures, and that (unlike 'history') it never quite escapes this primitive character, *unless subjected to a critical enquiry which is then integrated into the very structure of the experience offered. At which point the experience of 'heritage' becomes genuinely 'historical'*.

When, earlier in this writing, I suggested that a popular history (which I was linking to the heritage concept) partook of both 'real, concrete time' and 'mythic time' I was on the track of this idea. I would now, in the light of my case studies, wish to reshape that suggestion and argue that the succession of popular histories (and successive definitions of 'heritage') is the history of 'prefigurations'; and that since these are imaginative acts (White describes them as 'poetic' and 'linguistic') they are intrinsically unquestioned. They exist prior to any notion of explanation, and they are not in principle grounded in critical reason, but in commitment. This is, of course, a 'pure' form of heritage and more of an ideal type than a reality.

Seen in this way, 'heritage' is a celebration of the topics of history, rather than part of the activity of history. Furthermore, the acts of prefiguration are constitutive not simply of the field of study, but of the group that shares in them, just as popular history is also constitutive because it assumes the existence of the people or groups whose history it tells, and gives them identity in telling. Scholarly history, on the other hand, by disclosing its assumptions through self-critical reflection, is always in some measure 'deconstitutive'[1] or at least non-tautological. In principle, it admits of alternatives and has to defend itself.

In relating the idea of heritage to that of history we have to distinguish once again between two kinds of time. The struggle between real, concrete time and mythic time and the constitutive power of the latter is at the heart of the problem. It is not an abstract matter, but relates to a whole range of real-world questions of identity and action.

When Volkov describes the German 'mittelstand' as adhering to a 'collective memory [that] had little to do with the actual history of the craft guilds', and that this was a 'mythical view', she has to conclude that this actually helped to constitute them as a modern social group, whose 'imagined memory' became a 'fundamental instrument for shaping their future'; that is to say that the imaginative act had real-world consequences (see chapter 2). Furthermore, that modern social groups, no less than ancient, are constituted by shared 'mythical views'.

1. Scholarly history of course helps to constitute the group of 'scholars' – i.e. its participants.

By engaging with the idea of 'national heritage' we are imaginatively (and as visitors and tourists, temporarily) constituting the 'nation' (or region, group, industry, etc.) as a real entity, according to the underlying assumptions. We are, in play, enacting the creation and development of the concept of the 'nation', which (at least in nineteenth-century Europe) logically and imaginatively required its prefiguration in terms of traditions, languages, folk arts, etc. (because that is what then figured in the idea of 'nation'). To cast a critical eye over these categories is seen by nationalists as 'deconstituting' or 'deconstructing' the nation that is the ground of their cultural–historical position.

This does not mean that these traditions, folk arts, etc. (and clearly languages) are not real phenomena (though they are sometimes 'invented' or synthetic). Nor does it mean that nations are not real. They are recognised in constitutional law, in which nationality is defined in terms of birthplace, birthplace of parents, etc. Such definitions are legal and operational conventions adequate for their purpose. But it does mean that to ground the idea of a nation (or any other group) in terms of adherence to a 'heritage' is a kind of existential commitment for which it is not necessary to adduce evidence, except to exclude others. The principles of exclusion are intrinsic in the deepest and most primitive layers of the figured category.

We should consider, for example, how a third-generation individual whose forebears came from the West Indies or India responds to the notion of 'English heritage', even while describing herself as English. To what degree does she participate in this notion, if at all; and what sorts of 'English heritage' would it be with which she could happily identify. It would not be difficult to devise such, and very interesting they would be, but it would mean a drastic revision of what mainly passes for 'English heritage' today. The definition of x heritage is a way of defining who passes as x. And there is a dismal kind of competition amongst some Irish to determine who is the most Irish of all. The foreign visitor to a 'heritage centre' is invited into a temporary and (usually) benign collusion with these exclusion principles, as a privileged 'other'.[2] National examples are, of course, the most obvious, but all similar heritage is based on an exclusive definition.

The sinister aspects of exclusion need hardly be noted. In extreme cases, national heritage shades over into notions of national purity and 'ethnic cleansing' and racism, which always conclude in killing when the excluded are finally excluded from humanity.

In the case of Northern Ireland we may surmise that the forms of understanding that are used to grasp real, concrete differences, substantial inequalities, and actual social problems are underpinned

2. The degree to which any kind of uncritical collusion can be benign is a point for the philosopher of ethics. I assume here that tourism, and the cultural tourism that includes visits to 'heritage centres', is mainly a playful activity. But other cases do exist. It is not unknown for a tourist to enjoy an evening of 'traditional Irish music' only to find that he or she has been contributing to the funds of an illegal organisation; an artful strategy developed to a high level in the United States. And a participation in highly constructed versions of 'nationhood' is required of citizens in some regimes.

by a range of mutually incompatible acts of prefiguration. To describe the ensuing collision in terms of conflicting 'traditions' is inadequate, because 'traditions' are an epiphenomenon of much deeper commitments that cannot be reconciled. The language of invective used is often of the kind that would elsewhere be called 'racist'. A question that stood at the head of this little study – 'Whose heritage?' – is a demand for a constitutional answer in the full sense of the word. For there to be a reconciliation of opposing parties, there would have to be a new prefiguration of 'the North' (and therefore of much else besides) out of which new histories (and a new 'heritage') could in time be constructed. I give this brief example because it is the one that most concerns me, as an individual and as a citizen. Other examples, more or less extreme, come to mind. They demonstrate the link between representations of the past and acceptable forms of political legitimacy in the present. Indeed, we can say with confidence that it is not just history that is prefigured, but our understanding of contemporary reality. Constructing 'heritage' is a form of structuring the present, albeit in a fantastic or displaced form.

If I am right in assuming that 'heritage' (in its ideal form) is rooted in a preconceptual linguistic and poetic act of prefiguration *and that, unlike history, it finds it difficult to escape*, then it becomes much easier to understand the mythic elements that, appearing in representations of 'heritage', obstruct the free exercise of critical judgement. The 'figures' that are created – typically, but not exclusively, in the national past – are not truly historical entities but the headings or topics upon which histories can be written. They precede historical understandings, both in logic and in time.

This is well seen in the Ulster–American Folk Park, where a great deal of scholarship, detailed reconstruction and real historical research is enmeshed with a mythic progress-to-redemption. The kind of time in which the pilgrim crosses over into the Promised Land is that of perpetual re-enactment. The journey is lived by individual souls and by communities. These individuals are ourselves, in whose hearts the pilgrim-figure has arisen, (or, as visitors, ourselves taking on something of the same spirit of commitment and adventure through play): the communities are either the imagined groups of travellers in Bunyan's original stories (and the importance of friends, companions and family to the original pilgrim is an essential part of the meaning of the tale), or the real community of Dissent into which the visitor to the park is being temporarily and playfully admitted. This pilgrim-time is categorically distinct from the historical (real, concrete) time of actual emigration, and the experience of actual persons, which appear in mythic time as so many passing realisations of the immutable pattern. Events in this real time are open to manifold interpretations; but pilgrim-time cannot be inspected.

The appeal of heritage is based more than anything else upon this freedom from real, concrete time because to be held within heritage is, like the fly in amber, to be preserved from real time and from what Eliade describes as 'the terror of history' – the fear that human actions have no meaning, that wickedness is not punished, that there is no redemption and that we stand continually at the point of maximum responsibility and utter helplessness.

> Be it understood that we are not here concerned with the problem of evil . . . we are concerned with the problem of history as history, of the 'evil' that is bound up not with man's condition, but with his behaviour towards others. We would wish to know, for example, how it would be possible to tolerate, and to justify, the sufferings and annihilation of so many peoples who suffer and are annihilated for the simple reason that their geographical situation sets them in the pathway of history; that they are neighbours of empires in a state of permanent expansion. . . . And in our day, when historical pressure no longer allows any escape, how can man tolerate the catastrophes and horrors of history – from collective deportations and massacres to atomic bombings – if behind them he can glimpse no sign, no trans-historical meanings; if they are only the blind play of economic, social or political forces, or, even worse, only the result of the 'liberties' that a minority takes and exercises directly on the stage of universal history.[3]

3. Eliade, op. cit., pp. 150–1.

The concept of heritage – as developed above – holds out the false promise that something can be preserved that will not melt away in air, that is not subject to 'everlasting uncertainty and agitation' and which provides a transhistorical security. It is a secular version of the consolations of religion, addressed to the adherents of contemporary 'habitus'. The relation of 'heritage' to the headlong progress of modernisation becomes clear; it attempts a restitution. The appeal of heritage to a population undergoing yet another bout of the modernisation process (as is the case in both Ireland and Great Britain) is also clear; it offers the possibility (not entirely illusory) of maintaining contact with a vanished 'habitus' and keeping some sense of social continuity and valued difference consciously alive.

Though this lies beyond the scope of the book, the notion of heritage may also be brought to bear upon a much wider field, what McCandless calls the 'assumption that the cultures of the world have been radically displaced and fundamentally and forever altered by the movement of peoples'.[4] What is true in a small way for the comfortable reader may be true on the vast scale for all the uprooted of the earth. The universal penetration of industrial capitalism is producing a global culture of materials and media

4. McCandless (1992), p. 3.

that, spreading 'horizontally' around the world, closes off easy access to the 'vertical' dimensions of time, history and local/historical culture. McCandless continues:

> I read this displacement mainly positively, which is by no means the only possible reading. Specifically, I look to the radical hybridization of cultures as a precondition for the inventiveness and creativity which will be demanded from us all if we are to survive the epoch of the globalization of culture currently dominated by advanced capitalism.[5]

This is a position with which the present writer concurs, but I propose that we can best summarise the condition as an ensuing struggle between a 'sedentary' world experience, grounded vertically in place, history and slow change, and a 'nomadic' world of real or virtual travel, simultaneity and rapid change. This struggle *is* the present form of modern experience. In such a scheme, 'heritage' affirms one extreme; be it the small heritage represented to the cultural tourist, or the much greater heritage of religious faiths and racial solidarity. In its malignant form it contributes to an intolerant fundamentalism, which defends itself against real, concrete time by an hysterical recourse to mythic time.[6]

The malignant form of the further extreme – the raptured identification with the precession of imagery in a continuous present – is yet another form of assent to total authority.

In the time of real, concrete events, with which histories deal (be they in the form of annals, chronicles or scholarship, or as exhibitions, museums, etc.), facts and categories are open to critical investigation and can be abandoned or altered or transformed by that investigation, or by other real, concrete events. That is to say, the field of study can be subjected to a fresh prefiguration that makes new topics thinkable. This is how intellectual disciplines grow.

But a fresh prefiguration does not easily wipe out that which preceded it, and figures from the past continue to inhabit the present where they take on new meanings. A pertinent example might be the notion of 'Anglo-Saxon'. The authors of a recent and lively 'popular' history write: 'Like many myths, that of the Anglo-Saxons is fast becoming out of date, but it is curious and full of political and ideological undertones, not always in fashion.'[7]

L. and J. Laing identify a number of eras in which the 'Anglo-Saxons', who initially had 'little conception of national, racial or political loyalties', became the object of learned attention. In the eighth century, the Venerable Bede collected material and wrote the first history, at the point at which England had gained a political coherence under 'Anglo-Saxon' customs; in the twelfth, there was an increased interest in the legal documents of the time as part of the

5. Ibid.

6. Hence the appeal to eschatology in Christian fundamentalism, or the recourse to the 'eternal word' of the Koran. See particularly Salman Rushdie's novel *The Satanic Verses*, ch. 4: 'History is the blood-wine that must no longer be drunk. History the intoxicant, the creation and possession of the Devil, of the great Shaitan, the greatest of the lies – progress, science, rights – against which the Imam has set his face.'

7. Laing, L. and J. *Anglo-Saxon England* (London, Routledge and Kegan Paul 1979), p. 2.

increasing legalisation of the 'Anglo-Norman' state; and in the Tudor period, immediately after the Reformation, 'a search for the cultural identity of the English nation ensued, and in the 1560s scholars were feverishly poring over old Anglo-Saxon documents'. As part of a truly scholarly enterprise, a Saxon dictionary was published. (This was the period in which attempts to characterise a Celtic Britain were also begun, with the Tudor revival of Arthurian legend.) During the seventeenth and eighteenth centuries interest in Anglo-Saxondom waned, being beneath the interest of neo-classicism; but, like Celticity, it was revived in the early nineteenth century, both in scholarship and in historical fiction (*Ivanhoe* 1820), issuing finally in the beginnings of modern archaeology (J.Y. Akermann's *Remains of Pagan Saxondom* 1856). As part of later nineteenth-century imperial and racial theory the idea of Anglo-Saxondom contributed to 'a spate of propaganda which on occasions used historical and archaeological arguments to political ends'. This included ideals of Germanic brotherhood, the dialectic of 'Celt versus Anglo', imperial destiny, unions of 'English Speaking Peoples' (which excluded Caribbeans), and an extensive range of pseudo-scholarship. The penultimate stage was the designation of 'white Anglo-Saxon Protestants' by those who had been excluded from the benefits of WASP membership. Lastly, recent writers, like the Laings, have begun (surely correctly!) to reconstruct the 'Anglo-Saxons' in such a way as to merge them with all other groupings of the same period, emphasising the similarities and assimilation with 'Celts'. The Laings cheerfully admit that their account of Anglo-Saxondom is one which is more appropriate to the European Union. We anticipate an 'Anglo-Saxon Heritage Park' which, financed by European funds, will celebrate Hengist and Horsa as 'great Europeans'. In each and every case, a figure is being put to special, justificatory use in order to redefine the present and plan the future.

We can see from this and the exhibitions I have studied in chapter 5, that there is always a tension between the development of scholarly history and the need to sustain the prefigured ground on which, as upon a myth of creation, some social group or nation is identified. Popular history is the domain over which this tension is fought out, in every form of representation; be it in prose narrative, exhibition, theme park or film. At the one extreme the scholar deconstructs and dissolves whilst at the other the ideologue hypostatises and reifies!

This is why we should resist the reduction of mythical categories and explanations to the level of ideology. The mythical figures, be they persons, groups or nations, are the ground on which both scholarship and ideology interplay, and they are the longer-term guarrantors of the continuity of concepts that underpin social and historical continuity. Where, we might ask, would Irish nationalism have been without the notion of the 'Celts'; it would have been necessary to invent them.

And this general principle, as we have seen, is realised in particular cases. Once again, the Ulster–American Folk Park is a good example; the archival background, the loving reconstruction, the sense of detail are the product of real enquiry, even if the logical structure is mythic. Our journey through the park is informed by the intertwining of enquiry and assumption and we experience it as play, as a willed engagement not unlike that provided by a good historical novel, or a biography. No matter how grounded it is in scholarship, we do not mistake the novel for a history book. A similar process is at work in Studley Royal, where we are charmed into acquiescence by a site that has had its meanings changed by subtle manipulations of aesthetic effect. The brutal materials of history are made ductile by the picturesque.

The aestheticisation of history, however, has to be held at a distance; and this is the most difficult challenge which the serious creator of every heritage display has to overcome. Without that critical distance, aestheticisation leads straight toward the commodification of experience, and the assimilation of history into the commercial spectacle of late capitalism.

To recapitulate: I have used three headings under which to study aestheticisation. First, narrative topology, which is a form of emplotment. As in any narrative, there are devices of tension, surprise, association, and resolution whereby the material of the story is given form and impetus.[8] The degree to which these 'devices' are heuristic or inherent in the reality of the topic must be part of another study, but they are necessary preconditions of story-telling and one of the grounds of aesthetic experience. I note here that in employing the idea I have found it useful to use the 'story-board' technique such as a film director might use to organise sequences of film; and that I found the story-board method led to the concept of topology rather than the other way round.

Where visualisation is concerned, I believe I have established clearly the role of aesthetic concepts such as the picturesque and the sublime as modes by which we are led into an empathy with the topic; these are techniques of association. I think I have also established that a critical approach to historical material has to include a critical understanding of the visual representations of history and *a fortiori* a hyper-criticality with regard to their re-representation in 'heritage'.

Closely allied to the last, but not to be identified with it, is the practice of simulation. Here we are concerned with the concept of

8. See Hayden White op. cit., p. 7, *et seq*. As already explained, I have not attempted to use a strictly literary model.

the 'authentic' and the distinction between the real and the fake. The heuristic values of simulation are well established, and there seems to be no problem in the use of replicas in a *teaching* situation, but where heritage is concerned we are in a tricky area 'where scientific values may soon become indistinguishable from aesthetic ones, and where there is every likelihood that the aesthetic may dominate any scientific intention'.[9] The use of real persons in role-playing situations, as guides or story-tellers, raises the same questions.

9. Cook, Pat 'The Real Thing; Archaeology and Popular Culture', *CIRCA*, 56, March/April, p. 26.

What are the implications of this aestheticisation of history? I noted at the start of chapter 2 that the promotional literature of heritage exhibitions and parks transfers the language of tourism from travel in space to travel in time, and we have studied some of the means by which this temporal 'sight-seeing' is achieved; we have been offered our own or others' presumed pasts in the form of spectacle. The voyeuristic connotations of 'sight-seeing' are relevant, because the combination of simulated tableaux, narrative and visuality all come together in the obscene entertainment. Within a very few months of the invention of the daguerrotype it was being used for pornographic purposes; a similar process is at work in the electronic networks. Simulation (even historical simulation) is an ancient part of the brothel's repertoire. My suggestions here are not whimsical, but bear on essential features of contemporary visual experience. Feminism and psychoanalytic theory have accustomed us to consider the objec-tification processes associated with the gaze and the scopophiliac character of gender/power relations. My view would be that this is a secondary characteristic of the overall power of visual objectification which sight-seeing in all its ramifications (topographical, historical, erotic and more) induces. I mean by this that the power of objec-tification, which is prior to commodification, is immensely enhanced by those image-saturating visual media which now constitute the central ground of all contemporary culture. This visuality extends its empire over human geography through tourism, over the market through pictorial advertising, and over sexuality through the photo-graph. The heritage industry represents a further extension of the power of manipulated spectacle over history – as a direct consequence of its aestheticisation.

It would now be easy to conclude with a statement of cultural pessimism, which would take the arguments of a Jameson or a Baudrillard and align them – using only a little sleight of hand – with a neo-liberal economism to justify this state of affairs. Heri-tage would then become an assault upon our power of self-definition, a part of the wider commodification of experience. Identity, shared experience, history (and therefore the future) can no longer be main-tained in a world of contrived depthlessness and spectacle. Nor can it be otherwise; that is how it is (*etc.*).

Such an argument is easy to make and hard to refute. But against it I want to suggest a contrary case, arising directly from my case studies and from some of the concepts that I have been using.

In the broadest sense, to formulate the problem is the main part of its resolution. To understand the spectacular character of contemporary experience *as a spectacle* is to evoke its opposite, the values of reflective thought, of slow reactions, of patient and principled criticism. We come to understand the spectacle as an historical phenomenon itself, arising out of the first waves of primary modernisation (and described with such prophetic power by Marx and Engels); we begin to understand it in terms of its own technologies of image reproduction and endlessly inventive speculation, and to see those technologies as the generators of new understandings. We see that the retrospective glance, nostalgia and pastiche are not mere ephemera, but rooted in the real and long-term expansion of industrial society which, Janus-faced, has no secure home in any present time. They are what McCandless calls 'components of the conquering spirit of modernity – the grounds of its unifying consciousness'.[10] I have suggested that the true form of contemporary experience is a struggle between the 'sedentary' local/historical, and the 'nomadic' global/simultaneous extremes. If this is to be a fruitful struggle, then the two poles of experience need to be understood in a fully developed critical theory. One small stage in that would be the development of an appropriate popular 'local' history, which would balance the two forms of time. The study of heritage and its construction gives us a glimpse of strategies whereby we can both celebrate the past and gain a critical understanding of it.

10. McCandless (1976), p. 3. And see also Brett (1984).

Some of these strategies can be expressed as guidelines to both creators of and visitors to heritage displays. These guidelines are simple, even commonplace; but so are the first steps in any undertaking.

I think it has become clear that the character of the narrative topology in any one case can be of decisive importance; I propose as a general rule that a highly directed circulation, which cannot be reversed without embarrassment, should be suspected. Directing movement, it directs the process of inference and the patterns of association. There should be good and clearly expressed reasons for this, and the manipulation (for that is what it is) should be made transparent. In an exhibition that is openly didactic, or designed to demonstrate some thesis, directed circulation is likely to be appropriate, though we should expect this to be clearly indicated.

Where visualisation is concerned, similar principles apply (though it is hard to demonstrate them without pedantry). Visitors should be able to find out where certain images come from, how they were produced, under what conditions and so forth. Academic historians rarely understand that imagery is as slippery as text and needs acute critical investigation before being treated in evidence; and if scholars can't manage this, it is hard to expect the designers of exhibitions to do it for them.

Since we are compelled, by the nature of the task, to employ aesthetic strategies, then the classical modern prescriptions of 'making strange' and 'Verfremdungseffekt' should be studied.

One of the problems here is a typical design problem – the relation between the client's supposed intentions, the expression of those intentions in a brief, and the understanding of that brief by the designer and the creative team. One of the great strengths of the Strokestown Famine Museum is the visual coherence of the display which springs from the conceptual (and finally, personal) coherence of the group of people who put the exhibition together. There is a similar coherence about the Ulster–American Folk Park. It is notably missing at the Navan Centre.

Simulation, too, needs much more thorough understanding. The level of simulation (especially of human figures) is generally of a very poor technical and artistic quality, and carried through without much sense of style. A sense of style is much more important than it may seem at first, because the presence of style reveals the artifice and the play element in any display. It makes humour possible, and humour and the critical appraisal are close cousins. Humour and artistic exactness of expression are also closely linked and, giving pleasure, are great deflaters of the pompous. The delight that naïve people take in a skilful simulation should not be confused with a naïve understanding. (This is a point which neo-conservative critics of heritage and tourism completely fail to grasp; they think we are fools.)

These more technical considerations lead down to the deeper level of strategy, which is cognitive. We need to identify modes of understanding which, within the terms of a park or a display, are emancipatory. To return to the start of this study, our knowledge of history is not a fixed entity, but an activity. The more a heritage exhibition engages us in the exploration of knowledge, the more truly historical it becomes. There are several means by which this can be done. A non-directional topology invites us to construct our own 'narrative'; interactive displays (such as take place in the central section of the Navan Fort Centre) are an excellent way of exploring alternative explanations (especially for younger people); and the use of contrary audio-commentaries at the Famine Museum continually force us to reassess the visual evidence with which we have been confronted. Others can be imagined; but the strategy is always essentially one of confronting the visitor with alternative possibilities. In this way we, the visitors, create the integration and integrity of the experience; we are not given an 'interpretation'.

However, these alternatives cannot freely be grasped if they are hedged round with aesthetic considerations emanating from different fields of life. The proper place for the picturesque is in painting, not history; civil society is an attempt to expel the sublime from human affairs; denouements belong in the theatre. We admit them into history at the peril of them taking over, and turning real events into spectacle. And yet, at the same time, the very nature of narrative and imagery, without which history cannot be told because it is figurative, has an unavoidable aesthetic dimension. It is for these reasons that the spectacular element in heritage requires such careful handling.

As for alternative possibilities, given equal evidential and logical weight, I do not see that there are any grounds for choice that are not, ultimately, ethical decisions. 'The story that we tell ourselves is a form of self-definition and is therefore, and unavoidably, an ethical enterprise.' We must look to forms of popular history, and to a construction of heritage, that treats us as informed and ethical agents.

geography and heritage 3, 8
Gernsheim, A. 68
Gernsheim, H. 68
Gibbons, Luke 48
Gilpin, William 40, 42, 43, 59
Girouard, Mark 17
Girtin, Thomas 79
Godwin, E. W. 21
Goethe 138
Gothic style 26
Great Exhibition 1851 26, 63, 65,
    75–6, 81
Great Famine, the *see* famine
Greenhalgh, Paul 81, 83
Grimm brothers 55
guidebooks 43–4, 45, 46–7

Hadjiniclaou, Nicos 7
handcrafts 25 *see also* arts and
    crafts movement
Haraway, Donna 92
Harvey, David 12–13, 15 n2, 35
Heaton, W. 32
Henry, Grace 48
Henry, P. 47, 48, 58 heritage
    categorisation 154–5
    centres 34
    and culture 158–9
    displays 61, 163
    and geography 3, 8
    industry 1, 34, 162
    and landscape 49–51
    and modernism 8–9, 15, 158–9
    and myth 157–9
    and national identity 156
    nineteenth century 36
    Northern Ireland 2, 156–7
    parks, America 10
    and popular history 4, 7, 87, 155
    and post-modernity 9
    Scottish 17
    and the sublime 57–8
    and temporal tourism 15
    and time 155
Hewison, Robert 9–10, 12, 34
Highlands, the
    culture 17, 28
    idyll 83–4

and the picturesque 46
and the sublime 57
Hill, Chris 119
historical narrative 5
historical novels 16
history
    imaginative 33
    popular *see* popular history
    reality of 35
    scholarly v popular 160–61
House of Commons Select
        Committee on Arts 67
Houses of Parliament 19–20 *see
    also* Palace of Westminster
Hungarian architecture 27
Hungarian cultural nationalism
    26–7
Hyde, Ralph 79

Illustrated London News, The 73,
        74, 75, 142, 143, 144, 147
image explosion 63–4, 72, 75
image reproduction 61–72
imagery
    and modernism 63
    subliminity of 71–2
industrial modernity 15
industrial revolution 37
industrialisation *see also* printing;
        engraving 28–9, **30–32**, 36,
        59–60, 148
Ireland
    Connemara 45, 46–7
    picturesque and 38
    sublime and 38
    touring in 46
    heritage 1–3
Irish Museum of Modern Art 91
Irish nationalism 48
Irish School of art 48
Irishness 28
Ivins, William 71

Jameson, Fredric 34
Jennings, Humphrey 8, 15
Jennings, Jill 120
Joyce, James 34

Romantic subliminity 128–9
Romanticism 31, 53
Rosner, C. 65
Rousseau 45
Rowlandson, Thomas 44
ruins 42
Rural Tourism Movement 49
Ruskin, John 23, 24, 47–8
Russell, Benjamin 78

Said, Edward 38–9
Sandby, Paul 44, 60
Scarisbrick Hall 18
Schinkel, K. F. 79
Schnapp, Jeffrey 92
scholarly narrative 6, 114
Scott, M. Baillie 22
Scott, Ridley 126
Scott, Walter 16–17, 104
Scottish Exhibition of National
        History, Art and Industry
        1911 83–4
Sebron, Hippolyte 79
sense of space, post-modernism
        and 34
sense of time **29–31**, 34, 155
Sheehy, Jeanne 28
simulation *see also* exhibitions
    Ceide Fields Centre 137–9
    definition 87
    early examples 10, 11
    educational value 162
    Fountains Abbey 101
    Navan Fort Centre 124–5
    quality of 164
    Ulster-American Folk Park 107,
        115
    wax-work displays 85–6
Smeaton, John 72 n15
Smetana 27
Society for the Diffusion of Useful
        Knowledge 74
Society of the Protection of
        Ancient Buildings 22
Sorenson, Colin 14
space industry 60
spatial tourism 34, 162
spectacles 163

Spectator, The 63–4
Spielberg, Steven 150
St Giles, Cheadle 18
St Patrick's, Jordanstown 28
Strokestown Famine Museum 164
    narrative topology 140–42
    visualisation 142–50
Strokestown Park House 151–2
Studley Royal *see also* Fountains
        Abbey
    aestheticisation of history 161
    gardens 100
sublime, the
    and cultural nationalism 53–6
    definition 51–3
    and heritage 57–8
    and industry 59–60
    Ireland as 127
    and Navan Fort Centre 126–7
    Romantic 59 and scholarship
        55–6
    theory of 135
Synge, J. M. 55

Tate Gallery, London 91
Taylor, Warrington 21
technology
    change 32–3, 147
    of representation 61–86
    and sublime 59
temporal tourism 14–16
terrorism and tourism 127, 128
Tessonow, Heinrich 25
theme parks 117
Thompson, E. P. 32
timber housing 116
time
    pre-industrial 30
    sense of *see* sense of time
    and tourism *see* temporal
        tourism
Times, The 65
Topham, Samuel 68
Topolski, Jerzy 5, 6, 7, 114, 150
tourism
    cultural 127
    and the economy 1, 2, 3, 127–8
    and existentialism 115 n18